Africans and Negative Competition in Canadian Factories:

Revamping Canada's Immigration, Employment, and Welfare Policies?

Peter Ateh-Afac Fossungu

Langaa Research & Publishing CIG
Mankon, Bamenda

Publisher:

Langaa RPCIG
Langaa Research & Publishing Common Initiative Group
P.O. Box 902 Mankon
Bamenda
North West Region
Cameroon
Langaagrp@gmail.com
www.langaa-rpcig.net

Distributed in and outside N. America by African Books Collective
orders@africanbookscollective.com
www.africanbookscollective.com

ISBN: 9956-792-08-X

DISCLAIMER
All views expressed in this publication are those of the author and do not
necessarily reflect the views of Langaa RPCIG.

Table of Contents

Chapter 3: The Culturo-Colour Mixing Theories: African Nosexonomy, The Canadian Name-Game, And The Foreign Students Act On Parliament Hill.................**75**

Synopsis

According to Fossungu, we need healthy competition for progress. Competition that is not geared toward progress is negative competition. No competition or the absence of self-help is negative competition. With factories competing healthily, consumers have a variety of quality goods and services from which to choose. The entire community benefits when people in any grouping are competing positively; thus making the rules of competition graphical. The central focus of this book is the extent to which Canadian regulations apply without discrimination to *all of Canada* and to everyone, individuals and corporations alike. A swift answer is affirmative. But is that really it? The book is also about voluntary slavery, which is worse than forced enslavement. Drawing on *Ignorance Theory*, the book argues that the worst thing that can happen to anyone is to be ignorant of one's ignorance. He who does not know what he does not know will never know. Voluntary African slaves generally employ 'One Has No Choice' (*On n'a pas le choix*) to cloak their having chosen not to secure their rights. Fossungu demonstrates why he considers this an escapist way of shying away from doing the normal thing, thus giving the dictator or oppressor reason to dictate and oppress with impunity. This is Fossungu at his provocative and controversial best.

Introduction

WARNING! YOU ARE ENTERING **THE TRUTH ZONE!**

You do not hurt by telling the truth; it is the truth (that you have learnt to embrace) that hurts. If you learn to embrace the truth, you will seldom be hurt by it. This book, for example, could still have been written as a fictional story but I think that would be a big lie since I would be telling you my story without actually letting you know it is my story [Fossungu, 2013a: 1].

I remember being told by a literary friend in Nigeria that an excellent storyteller is one that keeps the readers always wondering about what they would be encountering next. That is, not quite knowing in what direction the writer is headed with them until they have actually taken the turn; or, as Jean Tardiff Lonkog's *The Black Man and his Visa* (2013) would have it, the book "keeps one wondering what will happen next."[1] Well, I am not sure that is what I have in store for you since I am not out to tell an excellent story, but a true one. If truth ends up being excellent, so be it; with all the glory being to the creator of the clock-ticking head of the storyteller. I have also been made to understand that to make a good critic or journalist you must not only ask your own questions but also anticipate and pose those of your potential audience. That instruction vividly brings to mind some cousins of mine. One was video-tapping during my mother's funeral in July 2014 and asked the other with whom they live: "Hello Sir, I don't know who you are. Could you introduce yourself to the Press?" The interviewee was kind of really mad, angrily asking "What do you mean by you don't know me?" before introducing himself as "Asah Fossungu Desmond…"

---

[1]http://www.langaa-rpcig.net/The-Black-Man-and-his-Visa.html

Many people begin reading a book like this one with preconceived ideas that the storyteller is on this or that side. That exercise might be futile here because there is only one side I am always on – that of a progressive and just society. It is normal that you want to know who this person calling for an overhaul of Canadian policies is and why this book is written. Free of all the book-filling titles, my name is Peter Ateh-Afac Fossungu. A Canadian of Cameroonian origin, I am personally incapable of hurting anyone. But my bitter truth does that 'hurting' all the time. I am known for embracing the bitter truth that many people can't just handle. That is even the main reason why I am still in Canada where I am hardly fitting in, and not in Cameroon where I *normally* would be, correctly educating the younger generation. I hardly fit in Canada not because I cannot fit into this great country. It is principally because Canada is yet to learn from the intriguing experiences and inter-cultural knowledge of some of its new citizens who, supposedly, do not have "Canadian Experience".

There is something though that I especially love about Canada generally and Montreal (in Quebec) in particular. I have had the privilege of going around Canada in numerous capacities. I didn't make the *Wild Rose Country* (Alberta) home since some Slavic-looking people there asked me to go *home* because they didn't know what a black man like me was there doing. It is a very long story but right now just know that I became a non-separating Quebecer instead. I don't exactly know what we Quebecers are always remembering on our own licence plate (*Je me souviens*), but I surely know exactly what this particular Quebecer talking to you is about to remember for *Yours to Discover* Ontario where Ottawa is located. I do hope you are keen and ready to explore '*The Unknown Country*' (Hutchisson, 1943) that has Ottawa as capital. Concerning its cities, Montréal seems to have a special flavour. That explains why it is the one Canadian city I have had to call home for a long, long time. Like most Canadian mega-cities, Montreal has it all. You just do not have to be actually living in any specific country of the world to be there. Live in Montréal and you can rightly boast of having lived the world over. 'I Love My Montréal' is the way we, *les Montréalais*, proudly put it.

In Canadian factories you will meet people of all sorts of national, ethnic, and racial backgrounds as well as varying educational levels. There are Africans, Asians, Europeans, Latinos (South Americans), etc., with those of you trying insistently to break all this down by nationality certainly getting lost in the exercise. Competition is everywhere every time and has become the sing-song. Johnny Tézano of Cameroon has sung his *Competition for Kumba* which is all about 'Money Palaver' (for women) and '*Njumba* Palaver' (for men). This book will be concentrating on negative competition with particular accent on Africans in Canadian factories, unique places from where I have learnt a lot on the subject. I think we need healthy completion for progress. Any competition that is not geared toward progress is regarded herein as negative competition. No competition as well is negative competition. Even the absence of self-help is negative competition.

If you are wondering as to whether negative competition is then unique to Africans, the best thing I simply can do is to direct you to Canadian *factories*. My use of factories is as pluralistic as it is extensive; being as stretchable as the capitalist definition of 'commodity' that captures even labour (see Sparke, 2013). I draw heavily from my *expibasketism* (or basket of experience) in presenting the facts herein, believing that expibasketism is best suited to helping anyone mastering it to be able to easily link up some dots that would otherwise be hard to connect (Fossungu, 2014b: viii). I do not quite know if the specialists would regard this uncommon science (or art?) as one that can be acquired or whether it is innate. But I know what one of them has told especially the Canadian authorities and Africans generally. Dr Rosetta Coding (of Examiner.com) in September 2013 did "recommend that sociologists, anthropologists, historians, and educators (all) lend an ear to Fossungu's writings" because "Peter Ateh-Afac Fossungu presents a means for Westerners to see African cultures and communities beyond the veil of the exotic and Orientalism", the author being, moreover, "an astute scholar of Canadian and Cameroon life" who "is objective in his viewpoint for most of this book" (Coding, 2013) Yes, you cannot but be objective when you are truthful.

Loudly calling for a significant revamping of Canadian immigration, employment and welfare policies, this book has four chapters. The first of them first introduces confusion before discussing the divorcé's dilemma. The second begins with putting much accent on the wanton employment of sex to enslave some *mbombo*-loving and unthinking people seeking 'papers' and resident status in Canada, a phenomenon that leads us to a look at children's best interests vis-à-vis Canadian institutions. Chapters three and four do very serious-funnily lighten up the heavily charged and difficult issues of race, sex and culture (discrimination, in short); topics that many people only love to genuinely talk about in the privacy of their rooms or hiding places. These chapters do so by plunging into the puzzles of race, sex, and culture; all the while drawing attention to the popular but little known 'Canadian Name-Game' in an effort to also defend the enactment of a Foreign Students Act on Parliament Hill. There is a no-conclusion conclusion, of course.

Chapter 1

The Mega-Rossy-Dynacast Connexion and the Divorcé's Dilemma: Divine Intervention with Momany Everywhere All the Time?

Differences and diversity, if properly managed, are supposed to be Africa's strength. The channel for properly managing them is federalism. But, rather than give the differences and diversity their proper channel that is called federalism, the Cameroon administration, for instance, only imposes the unitary state...The government's confusing policy is that of fanning the differences (for divide and rule purposes) but at the same time refusing that the two educational "sub-systems" responsible for these differences are different. This is simply being stupid since the differences are so deep-rooted and will not just go away simply because someone is trying to behave as if nothing was different. [Fossungu, 2013b: 90; omission has been added].

Introducing Confusion

This chapter has two parts. This first part introduces confusion while the second discusses Niki, children, sex, and the Botswana syndrome. Some call me the village-city, inter-continental, multidimensional person (see Fossungu, 2014a). When I write what I write, it is not just for the African audience. My writings are more useful to the non-African addressees, and especially Canadians – one of whom I am proud to be, even as I (with an incredible academic backyard) am still on the side-lines: thanks largely to the failure of Canadian institutions to grasp confusion. That is the whole *raison d'être* of my first book, *Understanding Confusion in Africa*

1

(Fossungu, 2013b). Talking of the understanding of confusion, some experts have largely attributed Canadians' lack of understanding of the confusion "to their failure to learn about what holds elsewhere (outside the USA, Europe and South-East Asia); a necessary learning that can greatly aid them in better understanding and appreciating what, as Canadians, they have. Cameroon is obviously one of those countries that Canada could be very carefully monitoring in this respect" (Fossungu, 2013c: xiv, note omitted).

I am hoping that in the course of my presentation of the plain facts in this book Canadians at large would also learn about some of the things they don't yet know. Especially concerning some of the myriad of contrivances that some of those (from other cultures) who reach the welcoming shores of Canada do employ to exploit the generous peoples of Canada. I hope my audience will exercise enough patience and understanding in order to get deep down into the heart of the matter, because I will understandably be a little longer on some of the issues and sharp-cutting (my trademark) in "pouring the stuff" in support of my points. The important thing, I think, is that the truth and nothing but the truth be made known. So, you are obviously asking, how does the divorcé fit in this truth-telling and learning process?

Divorcé in the title of this chapter brings the family courts to mind. Of course, I often go to Canadian Family Courts, but not to argue with the law that the Quebec and Ontario Bars tell me I don't know enough about. Hearing them say that, I doubt what you are here making of the Canadian universities in the Law Schools and Faculties of which I have arduously studied – Alberta, McGill, and Montréal. The Quebec Bar even went further to talk of my not being vest in Quebec's Civil Law, and therefore asking for my taking courses in any of the four universities recognized by them (McGill University, Université de Montréal, Université d'Ottawa, and Université de Sherbrooke), two of which I have already studied in! You would also wonder with me at this point if they are even aware of the Cameroon legal/judicial system that is predominantly, if not completely, Civil Law (see Fossungu, 2013b: chapter 2). Oh these Quebec Gang of Lawyers (or did someone just say Liars?)! They should simply have been frank enough to say they didn't want me anywhere near their Bar because I am too qualified and savvy for the liking of the 'charge and bail lawyers' (to use this well-known expression of Nigerian filmmakers) that the bulk of them are. Full stop.

I like the OQ (Over Qualified) reason that a few Canadian employers have used to justify not hiring me. That is more truthful, although that also means that some qualified persons like me would never work anywhere almost; not even in Aménagement MYR Inc. (hereinafter MYR). Thank you very much then "Mario Richard, propriétaire,"[1] who has in no insignificant way motivated (albeit unknowingly) the writing of this unique book. Some critics would argue, of course, that the 'OQ lovers' are afraid of being sued by the candidate after employment for being underpaid. Is that really so? I would then simply be a simpleton to voluntarily apply for a job meant for Master's holders and then sue to be paid as a Ph. D. holder. I guess such easy-way thinkers are waiting still for the day I will be suing MYR for hiring a Ph. D. holder as a *débroussailleur?* Order! Can we now leave these *gros titres* and get back quickly to Your Honour's court, please?

As I have said, I do not go to argue with the law in court. Canadian *experienced* lawyers are better placed to do that. I usually do not also have a lawyer. The women always go there to demand child support and I just cannot unwisely afford to pay the two. But I surely would be told by other Canadians that there is legal aid. Yes, of course. But we all know that legal aid

---

[1] You should note that in the place of Mario, Africans (with their incredible love of fabulous titles – see Fossungu, 2014b: chapter 1) will instead say, for example, 'Kadji de Fotso, Président-Directeur-Général'.

has its own limits and limitations. It has failed me before at a moment when I needed it the most. But that is not why I don't like having a lawyer in family matters. Not having a lawyer or arguing with them in court might not be a big issue because I don't really need a lawyer to tell me how to tell the truth. Telling the truth is a thing I have been doing from when I tumbled out of my mother's womb. The truth to be told here (in this chapter) begins with the factory called Mega Brands Inc. and rips through Canadian policies and institutions, including the courts in chapter 2. But I think a Haitian's theory would help put you in a comfortable seat for easy digestion of the truth in all the chapters of this unpretentious book on negative competition in Canadian factories.

A Haitian Theory, Funnyman, and the Outsourcing Device

The MYR camp in Dolbeau-Mistassini in Quebec is dominated by Burundians/Rwandans.[2] There is only one Haitian there called Lolo. I hope Ivoirians (three of them are in MYR) are not going to start thinking otherwise. This is not someone with breasts. Lolo is male. I have worked in Canadian factories that are completely dominated by Haitians, like Transit, a shoes distribution warehouse on Rue Hodge in Saint Laurent. If you are African and are with Haitians, always know that they are talking derisively about you: when you hear the word *misseh*. Some Africans have found Haitians to be the most awkward Blacks in the Caribbean. While a Jamaican (and most of the other English-speaking Caribbean nationalities pass easily for Jamaicans), for instance, would very eagerly associate with you (just knowing you are African), Haitians generally use

---

2 "It is hard for me to tell the difference between Burundians and Rwandans. I will therefore use Rwanda and Burundi interchangeably in this book as if they were the same" (Fossungu, 2014b: 7).

African as an insult. I wonder if they ever get Peter Tosh's message and also whether the only thing they know about Africa is that Africans are stupid slave-sellers. This *Haitianized* stereotype got to an explosive point on Rue Hodge, with a Nigerian and a Haitian locking horns arguing silliness.

The Transit Argument and Funnyman

The Haitian had gotten so bitter with the few Africans there because, according to him, the fore-parents of the latter sold their fore-parents into slavery. The Nigerian (trust them on this matter), on being aware of the thesis through my translation, quickly reacted. "I can perfectly comprehend," he told the Haitian, "why my fore-parents could so easily sell yours: they were the stupid ones. Otherwise, on being liberated, they should have returned to Africa, rather than jumping into a canoe and heading to a small island near the slave-driver! Or did someone tell them that Africa was so close by?" The laughter from the African side was very loud, obviously claiming victory for the Nigerian. I could not grasp what the two *voluntary slaves* were talking about, let alone ascribe victory to any side. Voluntary slavery is worse than the other well-known type, just as Native Reserves is worse than the well-known Apartheid: if you correctly put the 'borderless doctors' slant on them, as you should. It is a long story trying to specifically detail all that out right now but cut it short and clear with this brief *Ignorance Theory*. The worst thing that can happen to you is to be ignorant of your ignorance. As a teacher, my task is often made easier if my students know what they do not know. He who does not know what he does not know will never know. Funnyman will surely agree with me.

Funnyman: I have previously talked of people getting lost in trying to break the continents down by nationality. This holds not only because there are so many "funny" nationalities, especially in Africa, but also because of the difficulty of determination of those of some people like Funnyman. In the

MYR camp there is this interesting guy. He always has something interesting to say on every subject without dodging: except on the issue of what nationality is to be ascribed to him. Even his name cannot give me a clue since some of these Francophone West African names (e. g., Fofana, Diallo, Keita, Adama, Mamadou, Mahamadou) are clearly cross-border. I suspect the man is from one of those countries. But it is strange that none of the known Malians, Guineans, Ivoirians, Burkinabe, etc. in the camp do claim him. Even his French-speaking accent seems to be Central African (not that one country with Bangui as capital, but the *BEAC* region. BEAC is the French acronym for Bank of Central African States).

Discovering the guy's nationality has been without success. Maybe that is what makes him so funny, with so many funny nationalities on the continent. One different one every time you want to know, loving to be simply called *African*: his preferred nationality? I will just call him Funnyman in this book because it is generally accepted in the camp that he compares only with me in saying things others find funny. There was even a contest once in the camp between the two of us. They say Africans don't usually need humourists because they are always happy and laughing even in their *poverty* or *moneylessness*. But if you think that is still true with Africans in the West (shortened to *AITWs*) then think again! Funnyman and I often give the boys a good laugh, after the stress on the patches (*térrains*, they are called), either in the bus returning to camp or in the camp itself – this time with the white female cooks also sharing in the humour-fest. I beat him in the contest though because my '*juste pour rire*', unlike his monolingual one, combined several languages – English, French, Pidgin or Camtok, Amerench,[3] Kirundi, Swahili, Créole, Lingala, etc.

---

[3] For more on this North American language, see Fossungu, 2014b: 29-36.

There was much laughter that day (as on many others in the 'Forest School Bus' and 'Camp Kitchen/Restaurant').

Yes, get this clear. Africans themselves have proven that most of them are very good at laughing at their comedians and not what the artist is saying; nor do they even get the *fossungupalogistic* or trunk-cutting message. Hear them all over Francophone Africa laughing at Cameroonian Jean-Michel Kankan's sketches without any grasp of the man's messages. When are we going to listen and think and not just listen and laugh unnecessary? Did Nigeria really beat Haiti in the Transit Argument? Let the *Blackologist* in.

The Blackologist and Encore Automotive Politics

Haiti is, no doubt, the first independent Black nation and has produced some of the best minds the world has known. But I have not personally known any Haitian with the clairvoyance of one of them called Charly Julien that I met in Rossy Inc. Dollarama. (I will hereinafter refer to this factory simply as Rossy Inc. in order not to have it confused with the many Dollarama stores in town.) This Montreal distribution warehouse was on 5430 Rue Ferrier before, but has since moved to 5555 Royalmont, a street away. I would venture to style this Haitian a *Blackologist* or an expert on the comportment of Blacks. Charly once theorized to me as follows. *Prési* (that is the way they called me there, being short form for *président*), "if you go looking for a job in Montreal and get into a company where the majority or all of the workers are Blacks, you had better quickly withdraw your application." I *stupidly* asked to know why and Charly retorted: "Because, otherwise, you are actually requesting entrance into hell!" I guess what the Blackologist was saying here is to tell Matthew Sparke (2013) that, when next he wants to write about deplorable or sub-human working conditions in factories, he had better not fly from Washington State (USA) to China or to Bangladesh. He should just hop on a Greyhound and head

7

north to one of these Black-infested Canadian factories, saving himself a lot of expenses.

One of the dominant issues in this entire book has to do with whether Canadian regulations and/or laws apply *sans discrimination* to all of Canada and to everyone, individuals and corporations alike. The fast claim of the *Hypocracy* is often that they do. And for that the 1982 *Canadian Charter of Rights and Freedoms* and other employment, welfare, and immigration legislation are pushed in front.[4] Perhaps – just perhaps – that could hold in cities. But do Canada's vast forests constitute part and parcel of Canada, also meriting strict application of enacted regulations? Some people yet again would swiftly answer in the affirmative, with those of us in Quebec specifically citing the *Bureau de Normalisation du Québec* (BNQ), a comical body which Funnyman says actually means *Bureau de Niggerisation du Québec*. This man is indeed very funny (justifying his name too) but not stupid at all. I have unsuccessfully tried to make him tell me what he studied in school and to what level, with him often asking back whether he has to necessarily have gone to university and the like to acquire wisdom. That question observably always shuts me out of my 'cunny-man' discovery strategy.

But Funnyman appears to me to be more than correct in both cases. Otherwise, how does a Bureau actually normalize unfair competition (*la concurrence déloyale*, they call it in Québec) when its agents' visits to MYR are always made known to the MYR management before their arrival? It is the same with the CSST (Workplace Health and Security Commission) agents even in the factories in town like Rossy Inc., Encore Automotive, Royal International Corporation and the others. Is the prior announcement then not just meant for the

---

[4] "It is my view that the Charter, in its normal course, does not substantially rearrange society. In the normal course the Charter's benefits are, in any event, distributed in the same manner as legal services – preponderantly to the wealthy" (Whyte, 1992: 473).

"envelopes" to be ready for pick up on arrival? Next time you see me therefore just stop telling me that these unbecoming things are only done in Africa. That is fully empty bullshit, if the word has not already been over-worked like some of these stressed-up and lowly-paid African factory workers (or voluntary slaves) in Canada.

Encore Automotive Politics: The theses of both the Blackologist and Funnyman hold true, as I have discovered in several Canadian companies, including particularly Encore Automotive in Pointe-Claire (Montreal) and MYR in Dolbeau-Mistassini (northern Quebec). Encore Automotive, which produces all sorts of brake pads, used to be on 91 Boulevard Hymus before outsourcing to China. This is a device that tends to accord the capitalist more and more clout with which to abuse, especially using neoliberal networking of citizenship, strategies that Sparke (2013: 313-314) calls 'economic opportunism' and 'political exceptionalism'. Why don't they outsource to Africa too? A fifty dollar question! No one is interested in that. According to Steven Grosby, such outsourcing of jobs cuts three ways: (1) the allocation of production to geographically distant areas of cheap labour; (2) the importation of unskilled labour into wealthier countries to do unskilled work (so, this is Africa's part of the division of voluntary slavery?), which, of course, has been going on for some centuries now, both in the United States and in Western Europe; and (3) the importation of skilled labour from less industrially developed countries to the wealthier countries which is popularly known as "brain drain" (Grosby, 2005: 15). I would rather term all what Steven Grosby puts into 'brain drain' *voluntary slavery* too. The brain-drain phenomenon is usually attained through what Toft (2007: 143) protractedly describes as "Refugees as '*Diamonds*'".

All these processes, of course, do involve the movements of peoples across national borders, displacements that have no doubt occasioned stiff disputes over social benefits and the

9

granting of citizenship to immigrants, both legal and illegal, and perceived threats to the cultural distinctiveness of a nation (Grosby, 2005: 15; Toft, 2007; Hiebert, 2003). Examples of the response to these perceived threats to the cultural distinctiveness of a nation that the experts readily give include (1) a 1994 survey conducted throughout the European Union that indicated that 43% of respondents thought that there were too many foreigners (most of them being 'Refugees as *"Locust"*) in their respective countries; (2) the curtailment of the right to asylum in Germany through the amendment to Article 16 of the Basic Law (German Constitution); (3) restrictions on immigration and on the criteria for citizenship in France, and the attempts of the French government of Jacques Chirac to institute a policy banning French Muslim women from expressing in public their adherence to their religion by covering their heads in public schools – this also applies to Quebec under the recently defeated Pauline Marois government with its Secularization Bill; (4) unease in the United States of America over the widespread use of Spanish; and (5) the less-talked-about *'Sans Gate'* Africans-Tragedy of the 'Europe without borders' within the Transmanche region (see Grosby, 15; Toft, 2007: 143-145; Sparke, 2013: 323, 289-91; Hiebert, 2003).

You can thus see exactly what Encore Automotive is after, with its outsourcing to China, after what it has also done in Canada itself. I do not need to detain you very much further with its publicly hidden *Niggerization* politics, except to sum it up with the story that is told by its almost all-black labourers. How you enter Encore Automotive at the beginning of your shift as a white man and come out as a black man! So go figure out for yourself what you become at the end of the shift, entering there as a Black. While you do that, I will be taking you deep into the Mega-Rossy-Dynacast Connexion, beginning with mega half politics.

Mega Half Politics

Mega Brands Inc. is popularly known as Mega Bloks and is on 4505 Rue Hickmore. It is a leading company in Montreal in the fabrication of children's plastic toys. At the time I worked in Mega Bloks, I was living in a 11/2 apartment on 7110 Chemin de la Côte-Des-Neiges in Côte-Des-Neiges (CDN), quibbled by some critics like Funnyman as '*Côte-Des-Negres*' because of its predominantly black population and poor or sub-standard housing. Université de Montréal is partly located in CDN and, while schooling there, a female classmate asked me one day how much an apartment known as 41/2 in Montreal would cost in Cameroon. My response to her was: "I do not know because we do not have *half* rooms there!" In our beloved Quebec we talk of a 31/2 apartment, what Ontarians would be referring to as a 1-bedroom apartment. The difference between a 21/2 and 11/2 is a total mystery to me. I also wonder what in an apartment we Quebecers are calling *half*? Is it the kitchen or the washroom (bathroom) or what?

Whatever the half in the Québec apartment is, the significant fact is that when I applied to specifically work on the nightshift in Mega Bloks, it was not because I was jobless. It was a second job that I needed to be able to meet up with the financial pressures on me from all directions. It is usually easier to pick up a job in a factory for the night shift. This is popularly known as the graveyard shift, being one that not many regular workers would ask for. I was also not divorced legally, but separated, when I went to work in Mega Bloks. Nevertheless, in view of what had provoked my moving out of our spacious 41/2 LaSalle residence on 879 Boulevard Bishop Power to the small CDN apartment (see Fossungu, 2014a: 77 n. 9), mentally I knew I was 'spouseless'. After all, marriage is mental and has to do with the way the concerned parties comport themselves, not just the piece of paper and ceremony evidencing the status. That could also explain the fact that I was physically away from my wife for four years but did not consider myself as being without a spouse. You could therefore also capture my *spouselessness* here in Mega Bloks as divorced.

Apart from the Moulding Department, most of the company's departments are staffed by females from Africa, Asia, the Caribbean, and South America. From Africa (at the time I was there), Zimbabwe took the lead. This company is a notorious hub of negative competition. I am alluding to the fact that its supervisors and other heads exhibit a lot of favouritism in regard of their fellow 'continentals' or countries of origin. Most of these heads are Latinos and Asians. Africa has almost none. Why is Africa behind every other continent? Is it due to negative competition? Look at Nigeria (for example) that was once our own equivalent of the United States of America, with other Africans (including this writer) streaming into it, both lawfully and illegally, for greener pastures– just like the Latinos continue to do to the US. Nigeria has since fallen behind its Asian counterparts.

According to the experts, even Nigeria that was often regarded at one point as Africa's hope has declined like many other continental giants. In an article titled "Why Has Africa Grown Slowly?" Collier and Gunning (2013: 354-358) tell us that "Another good example of this divergence [of Africa falling while Asia, that had been lagging behind Africa until 1970s, is rising] is the comparison of Nigeria and Indonesia. Until around 1970, the economic performance of Nigeria was broadly superior to that of Indonesia, but over the next quarter-century outcomes diverged markedly, despite the common experience for both countries of an oil boom in a predominantly agricultural economy. Since 1980, aggregate per capita GDP in sub-Saharan Africa has declined at almost 1 percent per annum. The decline has been widespread: 32 countries are poorer now than in 1980. Today, sub-Saharan Africa is the lowest-income region in the world. " Of course, it could only get worse with globalization now hitting hard, with the stereotyping augmenting too. Why can't Africans see the simple and clear writing on the wall? Would their position in Mega Bloks (as elsewhere) not be reflecting it all?

In Mega Bloks, consequently, there is also plenty of ingratiation toward the heads and supervisors, coming especially from the African folks (females particularly). But the toadying trend just does not end with these heads, being particularly amplified by the obvious imbalance in the male-female ratio. I well remember two Zimbabwean ladies who seemed to have been praying and waiting for my arrival. I was not even assigned to the same spot as them but that was no impediment to their open and aggressive vying for me. Incredible Competition for Kumba! Am I the problem or them? I just hope none of them actually contacted home for any Africanscientific re-enforcements like the three drivers who went "to the village to get 'something' with which to finish me because they had thought I had used some charm to confuse the bulk of the passengers that were refusing to board their vehicles so that I could be the only one making the money" (Fossungu, 2013a: 81). You suspect this possibility because these ladies managed to be all over me, especially during breaks. What type of competition was this one looking like? Was I interested in any of them? Are they the divorced, and could they really be the Mega Bloks connexion? To find out, we will be looking at Niki, children, sex and the divorcé's dilemma in this chapter and Canadian institutions and children's best interests in the next chapter that also lifts the veil of victimhood.

Niki, Children, Sex, and the Botswana Syndrome

Sex is something many people like very much but few are willing to talk about it openly. Take a group of African men sitting together and drinking their *mbu*. Notice their reaction when a cock (to leave out dogs that seem to last forever)

13

suddenly climbs on a hen for the reproductive routine in plain view. See them all turning and looking away as if those fowls are crazy to be doing what they are doing. Yet, these are people who love the sexual act to an extent of wanting to have as many women as they possibly can. No waiting period when one woman is 'indisposed'. In a later chapter you will hear some of them in Ghana complaining about the white man and his religion that would impose on them 'one man one woman' "in the midst of plenty damsels." I am not here alluding only to that type of sex (intercourse) although it can hardly be completely cut off from the sexes that I have harped on especially in chapter 4. For now let us see what there is in there for the divorcé who may be of either sex.

Not being any of the aforementioned attention-seeking and aggressively competing women, Niki is this lady from Zimbabwe with striking personality and poise that only a man 'with liver' can defy. Yes, you need to be courageous enough because she has this peculiar gaze at you (as you approach) that seems to be loudly saying "Keep Off!" These are just the qualities that would instead bring Momany on "because of his *bigimprizism* (love for always going for the big or somewhat impossible prize)" (Fossungu, 2014a: 33). No need then for me to drag on designing Niki's beauty, but she was very motivated too. I can produce a sizeable volume just describing her motivation but let me also compress it here. She was my 'trouble' from day one. The day she finally accepted a ride from me I was enthralled. As we drove home that early morning, I inquired if she drives. She said she had her learner's permit, meaning she could not drive alone. I immediately pulled over and requested her to take the wheel. Only someone as motivated as Niki could have graciously accepted the unexpected offer. You will better grasp this issue if you understand my ex-wife's opposite view.

Schola was not even working then, but only studying, while I had to do two jobs to make ends meet for the family. She intentionally refused to prepare and go for her full licence despite that I had already bought her car. Her reason was that, if she had that licence, she would obviously be the one to be dropping and picking up the children at their day-care. She only went after that driving permit when she was about to leave Montreal for London, Ontario; hurriedly doing the driving around for it with her Cameroonian Bali female friend (Jennifer Semia Tita) with whom she was in the social work program in McGill University. You will find Flavie's similar or worse flaviqueenism in the second chapter or as also briefly described in Fossungu (2014a: 129-135).

Niki's performance behind the wheel was exquisite. You even get to appreciate it more after what she said later. That it was her first time ever taking the wheel (due to lack of the required companion). How come then that she was not at all nervous at the exercise? Her elucidation runs thus: "Perhaps, because you were not nervous yourself; your absolute confidence in this me that you hardly knew might also be responsible." As I was saying nothing, still savouring the discovery, she then added: "Peter, I feel very secure just being around you. I hope to be privileged to have this for a very long time. " Amen, I said; knowing now that she had gotten to where I wanted her to be – in love with me, as I had been with her since my first day in Mega Bloks. I had immediately informed Niki that the duration for her to go for the practical test for her full *permis de conduire* depended solely on her because, henceforth, she was driving us every morning to her home in LaSalle, from where I was to take over and head for Rossy Inc.

Niki just could not help regretting her not having accepted my offer to drop her at home the first time, before indicating that two weeks was more than enough for her to acquire her driving freedom. I was just as impressed by her motivation as she was by my encouragement. No one asked the other for a kiss, our first being spontaneous and so real. Ten days later,

Niki was requesting my special services. Could I have time over the weekend to help shop around for her car? Was that not a very special way of a special lady to let me know she had already obtained her licence? Of course, she meant business too because the following Saturday we were out together on a car-buying mission. Niki had instantly brought back the joy in me of knowing and having a loving, motivated and understanding partner. I was already in the gear to lovundelear (or love, understand, and learn from) her like I don't think I know what. You get to comprehend what I am talking about when you realize these facts. Niki is a single mother in Canada with three boys, ranging between fourteen and eight years (at the time), working nightshift. Having divorced her abusive partner in Zimbabwe (her version only), she immigrated to Canada to take the difficult and unknown bull by the horns. Niki was a complete contrast to Flavie (as seen in chapter 2) whom I met about five years after losing the former. I do not know if Niki's strange and abrupt departure from my life (just when things could only get better) was due to over love that quickly provokes unnecessary misunderstanding over children. I will give you the facts and you decide what it is or could be.

Punishing Devotion to Children?

Having been hurt so much by the man she so dearly loved and got married to, Niki had closed off men and love in her life for a long time. It is hardly astonishing that when she falls again in love with "a man that is very unlike other men" (her words), she falls so deep that any sign of deception should 'dooractionate the switch' (see Fossungu, 2014a: 120-122). And what was or could be that sign of deception? To Niki, it was my moving back in with Schola in LaSalle. Schola lost her father in February 2004 and travelled to Cameroon for the funeral. In the meantime I had to assume full responsibility for our three-year and ten-month children. It was not practicable for me to temporarily move the children and their stuff from LaSalle (where their day-care was) to my small apartment in CDN. In their mom's absence, I therefore had to temporarily stay with the children in LaSalle – while still maintaining my CDN residence. Niki just could not see the logic in this and read something else into my being back in LaSalle. Perhaps she would have seen reason if I had the necessary time thereafter with her at Mega Bloks. But I lost that job too since there is no official night-care for children. What must have been going on in Niki's head during the shift? Remember again that I worked during the day when the children would be in day-care and Niki (who would not take calls) was at home resting. I therefore lost both job and friend because of my devotion to my children. Painful does not begin to describe it sufficiently.

Here are some questions. Should I be in Montreal and someone else be taking care of my daughter and son during their mother's absence, simply because I had moved out, and to please and keep Niki? Is this issue peculiar to this particular case or is it a common trend with divorced people with children? Does the fact that parents are separated or divorced have to meddle with their relations with the children? It was nothing close to chantadelamatism (where there was obvious competition between Chantal and Adela – see Fossungu, 2014a: 112-115). But why did Niki choose negative competition instead than actively compete (fight) to have me, if she really loved me as I thought? I ask this question because you already know that no competition and lack of self-help are all forms of negative competition. It is just like this guy who claims to love the Cameroon presidency so much but would not venture to compete with 33-year-ruling Paul Biya 'for the sake of peace'. Has there ever been real peace without a fight/struggle/war? That is what I castigate as politickerization or the fear of politics (see Fossungu, 2014b).

Anyway, if Niki did fight, I am sure I would then have had the chance to let her know she was actually in no competition with Schola for me. Things would then have been very different today; for, as I have said over and over, positive competition begets progress. Niki clearly had that opportunity then to have prevented me from meeting Flavie and many other women between them. As you should know, Flavie is the lady that five years later filled the vacuum left by Niki, who relocated to Brampton in Ontario even before Schola returned from Cameroon. While I met Niki already working in Mega Bloks, I was the one who personally looked for Flavie's job there. But Flavie never actually worked there because she was to commence the next day, bringing along her work permit. It was on reaching home that evening that she discovered the permit had long expired. There is already much on her flaviqueenist attitude (see Fossungu, 2014a: 132-135), but the second chapter focuses on her recent May 2014 court suit for custody and child support that is wrapped in the blanket of victimhood. Children are always being used to cover up egoistic agendas. Was Niki too not actively competing because she was afraid of failure: taking my having children with Schola as an advantage over her who was just coming into my life? Is this issue too just unique to the duo here or a common problem with divorcés wishing to remarry? Was it indeed compulsion in love or the Botswana syndrome?

Compulsion in Love or the Botswana Syndrome?

I gathered before that Niki could be very compulsive when she loves her thing. But not to the extent that she would behave as she did in the *Moving in Affaire*. When Niki and I were shopping for her car, I was supposed to do the pricing. At the time Zimbabweans were noted for all going after Chrysler Intrepid, *sous-nommé* Zimbabwean Mercedes. We found the car she loved, a black Chevrolet Cavalier. Despite the many rejections of Japanese cars that I had suggested, I was impressed with her choice. After all it was *her* car. (Schola too had chosen a Chevrolet Lumina, ignoring my suggestion of a Toyota Camry but has since leaving me been so faithful to Honda, going from Civic to CR-V.) The salesman told us the Chevy was going at $4000. 00. Before I could start bidding, Niki had accepted taking it at the price. This is a car that I would normally have bought for about $2500. 00. As she explained to me later, "Why should I not obtain what I like when I have the cash?" Do you just have to spend money unnecessarily simply because you have it? Do you also have to eat a "Mountain" of unhealthy food just because MYR deducts its fixed cost from your pay?

Some MYR workers (particularly a Cameroonian called Lazare) are culprits in this kind of thinking. These heavy-eaters even always go over and over "repeating" MYR's *griotte* that several workers don't even eat. I am adopting 'repeating' here from a Zairian who told the cook's assistant who was serving us food that *"Je vais répéter le manger-là parce que c'est vraiment bonne!"* (I continue to stick to Zaire rather than Congo to eschew confusing the two Congolese) These days in MYR people no longer say 'I want to eat again or have a second dish' but instead 'I want to repeat the food' *à la Zairoise*! So, what is this meal that others are 'repeating' while the majority is not keen on eating? *Griotte* could be equated with what Cameroonians popularly call *pap*, which is locally made from corn. *Griotte* is from wheat though, including what others would be referring to as Quaker Oats. I eat oats at home but not MYR's *griotte*, like most others there, notably another Zairian who is behind the Zairian Hang-On Rule (as to which rule, see Fossungu, 2014b: 141-48). What is added to it in the course of its preparation, no one knows. Others would not explain why they have stopped eating the stuff but Funnyman does not shy away from any of these things. According to him, he put an end to it because it was detrimental to his output on the field. Instead of cutting his *un térrain*, he would spend most of the time dotting it with his *'purge-belly-shittings'*! His advice to

19

us therefore was that we should eat plenty of MYR's *griotte* especially when we haven't done a good job on the patches and intend to avoid being slammed with *réprises*. Of course, most *contremaîtres* hate to repeatedly step on *ka-ka* when they *marcher un térrains* (or cross-check if it is finished and well done). Could that be the secret of MYR's so-called *grands coupeurs* or very experienced tree-cutters discussed by Fossungu (2014b: chapter 2) most whom are heavy *griotte* consumers?

Was there also a secret being divulged by the Montreal car-buying enterprise as well? Put differently, I wonder why I was at that car-buying show with Niki: just to drive her or as someone knowledgeable with cars and who could help her from being ripped off by unscrupulous car dealers? Does this quite look like the "my way or no way" lady? Was I too blind not to read the writing on the wall? But would you really be in love if you read too much into every act or word of the other? Wouldn't that have transformed you into a real schemer rather than lover? A real lover, I think, would fight to keep his/her loved one, whether or not the need for competition is clear. Or, can the Botswana syndrome explain Niki's actions? That is, is Niki really from Botswana, and not Zimbabwe?

Cameroon apart, I have never lived anywhere else in Africa except Nigeria. But I have this admiration for Botswana, especially for the academic refuge and freedom it has provided in recent years to a host of University of Yaoundé (UNIYAO) mentors and colleagues that the regime in place says must not teach students in the manner it has to be done. Thank you Botswana and Southern Africa generally. When I read the numerous comparisons of Botswana and Cameroon, as offered by Fombad (2005; 2003), I cannot but be moved. But that is not why I am now moved to discuss the Southern African country with you. I am here solely relying on some second-hand echoes gathered from two Canadian factories. The first is called Rossy Inc. (already seen) and the second is Dynacast Inc. which was in Pointe-Claire. Claiming to be the world's largest die caster, Dynacast produces several items (for automotive, consumer electronics, and telecommunications manufacturers) from melted aluminium especially, including chin and moustache shaving sticks. This company, like Encore Automotive, also relocated in mid-2010 to its new plant in Dongguan in Southern China.[5]

Collins is my educator on the matter. He is a very hardworking Zimbabwean who is married to a lady from Botswana. He and I worked two jobs together in both factories for quite a long time, about two years. While I was a *titulaire* in Rossy Inc. and worked in Dynacast through an employment agency called Première Personnel, Collins worked in both through two different agencies – Service de Personnel Serviko Inc. for Rossy Inc. and Première Personnel for Dynacast. We were pot-men who work the night shift (11 PM – 7 AM) in Pointe-Claire from where we headed together (in my Audi car) to Royalmont for the day shift (7. 30 AM – 4. 00 PM). The position of pot-man is one of the most demanding and dangerous in Dynacast. Only people (mostly Blacks) sent in by the agency handle this job. The other employment agency that also sent workers to Dynacast was called TP Magzin. It brought in mostly Asians who were assigned to only sorting and other table-centred jobs. The pot-man job involves not only filling aluminium bars into the pots but also routinely cleaning by taking out the unwanted foam-like stuff from the many extremely hot "pots" from where the connected die-casting machines get their "feeding" for whatever customer orders that are being manufactured.

In addition, the regular company workers (*titulaires*, they are called) tending the die-casting machines just would not realize that inhaling all that harmful vapour is more than enough. As you try to catch your breath after a round at the pots, they

---

[5] See http://foundrymag. com/materials/dynacast-shifting-production-new-plant-china.

would order you around to do this and that until you are back to the pots again. Collins and the others succumbed to that, not this me. I got my freedom from day one when this 'full-of-himself' Filipino tried the ordering-around. I asked him if he had schooled enough to know what *pot-man* means. "That means I tend the pot and nothing but the pot", I taught the guy from The Philippines. I wonder if a woman can stand this job; and if so, would she still be called pot-*man*?

The job is quite risky but even more fatal for someone like Collins who does not sleep well during the day/evening. Imagine falling into that pot because of sleep! The only sleep the man gets between his shifts is in a shift. Yet, he is just as adamant on not playing by the Rossy Inc. Moroccan supervisor's oppressive rules as he is uncompromising with anyone who says anything positive about President Robert Mugabe. I do really think a critic's incisive point on Karl Marx almost completely paints the Collins-Mugabe thing. According to Eagleton (2011), "Praising Karl Marx might seem as perverse as putting a good word for the Boston Strangler. Were not Marx's ideas responsible for despotism, mass murder, labor camps, economic catastrophe, and the loss of liberty for millions of men and women? Was not one of his devoted disciples a paranoid Georgian peasant by the name of Stalin, and another a brutal Chinese dictator who may well have had the blood of some 30 million of his people on his hands?"[6]

---

[6] By the way, has 'western civilization' also been condemned *in toto* simply because it has its Nazis, Ku Klux Klan, not to mention its so-called justification for and practice of slavery, etc.? One would say this because "The truth is that Marx was no more responsible for the monstrous oppression of the communist world than Jesus was responsible for the Inquisition" (Eagleton, 2011). No one is here playing advocate though; just the unbiased judge that academicians should strive to be. "Academic economists," Rodrik (2011: 63-64) has also counselled, "are rewarded for divergent thinking and being innovative. That includes identifying different ways in which markets fail and crafting new arguments for how government intervention in the economy can make things better." Wouldn't a communist pope, for instance, be able to perform better than those we are

The Moroccan's illicit demand of twenty dollars every week from agency workers, to Collins, was a thing he would never submit to because not only was it exploitative but also he (Collins) was not then "working under the table". Why not just pay and get peaceful sleep like other two-jobbers then? No. Collins stood firm and got away with momentary sleeping, having threatened the harassing supervisor with exposure, should the supervisor continue to disturb him. But could he have slept enough at work? And why was he having no sleep at home?

Debunking the Collinsian Theory: Sex-Slaving or Marriage?

Collins had the same (or even worse) home problems like me, resulting from an exploitative and inconsiderate spouse. It is a very lengthy story that can constitute a separate book of its own. But I once wondered to Collins why (unlike me) he was there talking all the "shit". Quite apart from their having a daughter he loves so much, Collins admitted that he just could not afford leaving the wife. Why? I can see you are in such a hurry to know. It is on the way coming and coming to shock you: "The sex I get from her I can't get from anyone else." Really? Oh this SEX: Send Every-thing to me or X (your destruction)! Was Collins in love with the woman in the first place or just with the sex? Why wouldn't he say NO to the exploitation here as he did to that of the Rossy Inc. supervisor? This is a very interesting question that leads us to debunking confusion, being fully loaded like some SUVs (Sport Utility Vehicles), notably the American Buick Enclave that is very

---

used to? Just posing this question, to some people, is equivalent to breaking hell loose. As Lindorff (2013) says, "That's quite a lot for many Americans to swallow. For someone like Rush Limbaugh or Fox commentator Andrew Napolitano, it must feel like the world is collapsing. A 'Marxist' pope! How could God allow such a thing?"

indicative of mobile reterritorialization in a so-called 'borderless world' said to have been created by globalization.

The processes and forces of globalization have greatly augmented in recent decades due especially to advancement in technology. This technological revolution has obviously shrunken time and distance in unprecedented ways, permitting globalization to surmount some of the obstacles associated with 'the territorial trap'. Nation-state borders may be becoming less and less important in the face of increasing globalization. But that does not mean that deterritorialization has necessarily created a 'borderless world'. Also commonly known as 'The End of the Nation-State' and 'The End of Geography' (see Toal, 1999; Paasi, 2009), the heralded deterritorialization process has indeed, on the contrary, been reterritorialization, punctuated with accentuated uneven development and other forms of immense inequality. Such an end-product can scarcely be appropriately termed the creation of a 'level-playing field' or 'borderless world' by globalization. What is clear is that "globalization creates new tensions and divisions as well as new forms of global integration" (Sparke, 2013: xiv). As such, simple sound-bites about globalization's creation of a 'borderless world' would essentially be a calculated neoliberal denial of "the historical waxing and waning of uneven development" (Sparke, 2013: 288).

'Border' and 'territoriality' look like synonyms and are used as such by many globalization writers. But political geographers would indicate that these terms also have their specificities. Otherwise, there would be no need for Paasi (1999: 216) to be talking of "the marriage between territories and borders [which] is impregnated with societal power, so that it continues to be crucial to reflect on how these elements come together in the practice of territoriality. " Make the necessary substitution here for 'territories and borders' with 'penises and vaginas' and for 'territorialty' with 'sex' and you have got the perfect power-game in the *Collinsian Theory* or the *mbombo* trap, a funny trap that is more elaborately analysed in the next chapter.

Territoriality thus involves much more than borders and territories. The 'borderless world' theory cannot therefore be correctly grasped without a good understanding of the meaning of *border* "since much of the current ambiguity and either-or arguments regarding the disappearance of borders seem to emerge from a rather fixed idea of what borders are and where they are 'located'" (Paasi, 2009: 215). Anssi Paasi hits very hard at the core of the problem, but it is not only important to properly grasp and locate borders. Equally crucial is Toal's (1999: 149) advice that 'borderless world' discourses be necessarily "problematised by old political economy questions: Who benefits? What class promotes the discourse of 'borderless worlds'? For whom is the world borderless?" These are very important issues to bear in mind as we attempt to comprehend the persistence of borders and/or boundedness in an unbound world. In doing so, therefore, "borders should not be seen solely as phenomena located at the 'edges' of territories but rather 'all over' territories, in innumerable societal practices and discourses" (Paasi, 2009: 215). Thus, borders or boundaries must not be restricted to just 'national' ones but must extend to 'Enclaves, Slums, and Citizenship' (Sparke, 2013: 313-333; Toft, 2007; Debrix, 1998); as well as to the neoliberal distortion between "disputed border" or geopolitics and "free trade region" or geo-economics (Sparke, 2013: 289-97; Savage, 2014).

You see just how far and rapidly our Buick Enclave has *reterritorialized* us away from Collins' unsavoury justification for not playing by the twisted rules of the Rossy Moroccan Monarch? The plainest of facts is that Collins simply could not pay for sleep because all what he made doing two jobs went completely to paying for the SEX(Save Everything for me or X) that he thinks he cannot get elsewhere. He did not see nor touch the money he earned; it was the 'sex-seller' who did, making sure of course that he had always just the bus pass for the week. You need to have seen what Collins often ate at work, just because of sex or *mbombo*-love. Other workers' scrappy leftovers! I wonder what he would have done in the place of a Nigerian (in chapter 2) who was to have all the sex (*toto*, as Naja-man himself calls it): provided he did not get out there to work in 'official' Canadian factories, the working white woman providing for him just enough to keep fit for the sex-machine role.

But Collins tells you everything he knows, knowing that he cannot disentangle himself because Botswana women are very good at using what Cameroonians call *gri-gri* or charm. It is a cult with them, he explains. It begins when a girl is born in Botswana. The child is never put to bed lying on the back, but face down. Why take such risk of suffocating the child? For the desired development of the enticing and huge makandi which, like Charlotte's in Charalicism, gets the men to speedily erect (see Fossungu, 2014a: 30). (Niki obviously was not lacking in this makandi or huge buttocks business.) There are many other rituals that follow through until the *grand finale* which occurs during the first sexual encounter with the target, at which time he is logged in and locked up. That was the Gospel according to St. Prisoner Collins, gospel that raises some questions about my ever-dear and missed-a-lot Niki's comportment.

Questions on Niki's Comportment

Why do most people from Botswana out here in Canada easily and readily pass for Zimbabweans? Is it possibly for the easy claim to refugee status and/or a means of avoiding the noted syndrome? Why was Niki not associating much nor behaving like the other Zimbabwean ladies in Mega Bloks? It is not like I was so sex-starved and hastily wanted to perform "[t]he second purpose for marriage [which] was the control and channeling of the sex drive" (Jungling, 2007: 68). Had sex been the sole issue, the two fierce competitors would easily have *rempli la tâche.* But why was Niki sort of postponing and planning to make our first sex "something to remember"? Why was she ready just when the obstructing Cameroon death and journey occurred? Is this another Divine Intervention again, perhaps? In other terms, was someone out to prevent my being logged in and locked up? Why also the hasty and unannounced relocation to Ontario? Why? Why? Why? About this Niki that I fell for *sans glisser*, there are questions and questions and more questions. But that was not all there was to this moving woman that I was already calling mine. Her other unique characteristic, *nosexonomy*, is discussed in chapter 3. But the road to that chapter passes through chapter 2 that also examines the lady that eventually replaced Niki and is now brandishing her illegitimate victimhood card.

Canadian Institutions And Children's Best Interest: Exposing The Mbombo Trap And Lifting The Blanket Of Victimhood

Westermarck then contends that the development of marriage among humans was less about the relationship between the husband and the wife and more a matter of raising offspring. Thus there are other theories about the origin of marriage that suggest that marriage was a way of ensuring that procreative activities would be successful which would in return increase the likelihood of survival for all men, women and children [Westbrook, 2010: 12].

I was in court in May 2014 not to argue with the law but solely to assist the law (on which the judge is an obvious expert) to reach a just decision; one that places the paramount interests of the children above all machinations from whatever source. By children here, I do not mean just the two kids named in Flvie's *wholly unnecessary* suit. For these children's interests to be appropriately guaranteed, therefore, it was my view that the Court was entitled to (and had to be given) all the essential facts, not the appearances. Against that background, I will therefore mostly be spending time in this chapter acquainting you with **HOW/WHY** we got to being in court. But before I get to focus on that, permit me to indicate right away that I think that continued shared custody best serves the children's interests.

Shared Custody V. Full Custody: Two Essential Questions For Fighting For Children

There is obviously a war between these types of custody over the concerned children. This portion of the chapter thus

29

examines two essential questions that are required for successfully fighting for the best interests of the children. *Two simple questions* really needing to be examined in regard of the two children (Peter, Jr. and Peteraf) are: (1) *Why does Henriette Flavie Bayiha want to have Full Custody of them?* The uncomplicated response is clear: Just for the money; and money which she will not spend on them but instead to send to Cameroon. Otherwise: (a) She needs to have first satisfied the Court that she has regularized her situation in Canada (the why of her situation, will be seen below), since (b) She cannot have full custody of the children while expecting me to be signing day-care and other contracts – agreements that she would not respect anyways (as to be also fully seen below). I am here therefore calling on Canadian Courts and other Institutions nationwide not to continue helping some parents to "use the children, knowingly or otherwise, to further their own selfish agendas, not bothering about the child[ren]'s own feelings, interests and future" (Fossungu, 2013a: 152).

(2) Why does Peter Ateh-Afac Fossungu (Sr.) want to continue with Shared Custody of the children? His stance is solely for their best interest and future. That is why I made it clear that should the Court find that one of us **must** have full custody and, say, it was me: I was asking for no money from Flavie whatsoever, whether or not she starts working (and why must an able-bodied adult like her not be made to fend for herself?). I take this stance because I believe that if Flavie truly loves her children, first, we wouldn't have then been in court and, second, she wouldn't need a court order to do whatever she wants to financially do for them. Also, I still earnestly want to help the two children (Lindsey Hervée Bayiha and Scott Alexandre Bayiha) in Cameroon that their mother has so far very unthinkingly prevented me from aiding, as seen in the paragraphs below. I believe that the Court properly owes these two innocent children a duty to make sure that they get the help I want to give to them, over and above the head of their

mother who cares less about anything else but her egoistic schemes.

Fighting for the Children: Flavie's schemes are solely geared to get her into social welfare. She has the right to whatever she wants to do with her life but I think our children should be left out of her schemes. If that was her intention, it was clearly never mine, to bring children into this world for Social Welfare Service to raise them while I am alive and kicking. I have been happily paying arrears of child support that accumulated when I was out of work. It was normally not supposed to get to that point. But it got there all the same because of a similar conniving demeanour. I pay not just because of the law but mostly because it is my responsibility to raise my children. If I have been ready and willing to take the same responsibility and care for the two children that Flavie has with someone else in Cameroon (children that, it must be noted and emphasized, I have not yet even met), there is no convincing evidence to show to the Court or anyone else that I am unable and unwilling to take responsibility and care of my blood children: whatever the woman I have them with, Flavie included.

I therefore always stand in court not only as the mouthpiece of voiceless children, but also here talking "from the viewpoint of a parent who is concerned about the way some parents are using children as mere means of acquiring revenue from or tools of punishing the other parent; and they persist in doing so to the total disregard of the future of said children who paradoxically do not even feature in their un-African and un-Canadian definition of family" (Fossungu, 2013a: vii). In the final analysis, as I must be emphatic about it, "A child must not be considered a child by the parents only insofar as the child's services [in the form of the money s/he brings in] are concerned but regarded not as a child when it comes to the education and other [emotional] needs of that child" (Fossungu, 2013a: vii).

I believe that all these children are entitled to have both parents (whom they had no choice, like us parents, in choosing) in their lives. For about four years I have done everything any reasonable and caring person would do to work hand in hand with Flavie for the betterment of us all. But it has been unfruitful because it is very hard to help a nonoselfist or someone who only believes that he or she is entitled to sit around and do nothing other than to be on the phone 24/7 while others do everything for him or her. And yet it is amazing that such a person gives no bit of respect to those doing those things. As already and will continue to be noted, I have been there more than once and can therefore tell the bitter truth better. Flavie is the most disrespectful person I have encountered in my fifty-four years of life. I would really appreciate seeing that other person that would be able to (cohabit with her and) tolerate her comportment for even one-tenth of the period I have.

Of course, I cannot stand her anymore as a partner but that does not and cannot change the fact that both of us remain parents to the children, and must work together for that purpose. And, luckily for me (and the children too), I am bitter-free since I always embrace the bitter truth that often renders those who cannot hug it bitter. In addition, and as a consequence of the foregoing, I have learnt to separate things and deal with them accordingly in a balanced or even-handed manner. That skill or 'comportment science' is called crisebacology (see Fossungu, 2014a: 24-29). But for my being blessed with this rare skill, you can rest assured that I would not be the one still talking marriage and children after Schola's unexpected re-definition of marriage when, through my singular efforts, she set feet on Canadian soil. Children are entitled not to be entirely left with a bitter and/or scheming parent, and I am pleading and hoping that Canadian Courts are not going to continue failing Canadian children like the Ontario Court apparently did to two Quebec children in 2006.

Therefore, if the Quebec Courts are interested in the paramount interests of the children, I had made it clear, let them tell me what financial contribution to make to Flavie during the months when I am (and have been) away from Montreal, all in the business of trying to secure a guaranteed future for them. I further pleaded with the Court to tell me anything other than that it was letting Flavie have full custody of the children that she is merely using for her schemes. No matter how much I disagree with her free-riding comportment, I have never intended keeping her away from our children. Also, my paying child support is not the issue; it is the question of what is best for the children. The facts to support these simple claims now follow, beginning with (1) capagivism and the mbombo trap that leads to (2) the imbecilic passing for a victim.

Capagivism and the *Mbombo* Trap

Capagivism, as you are about to discover, is a sort of playing around with the institution of marriage, one of whose purposes "was the social purpose, through which men and women fulfilled their roles in and for society so that order and peace could be maintained" (Jungling, 2007:69). Westbrook's doctoral research shows that marriages are failing and the institution of marriage as a social institution is declining in North America. Similar research suggests that trends towards non-marriage, cohabitation, and divorce are practically the same among Christians and non-Christians. Neil Westbrook does not think the role of the local church in this situation is well understood. He therefore opines that while there are many assumptions about the relationship between the local church and marriage, clearly the role of the local church in marriage needs further examination (Westbrook, 2010: 6).

Some of the experts have thus gone into researching the issues especially because current surveys and polls suggest that

33

about 50% of all currently married couples in America will divorce. Considering that more and more people are not getting married, that the total number of out-of-wedlock births is steadily rising and that more adults of all ages are cohabitating, it is clear to Neil Westbrook that marriage as an institution is failing in society. According to him, the reasons for these trends and the decline of marriage are many and complex; with leaders from multiple disciplines - religion, politics and sociology - having joined the discussion about why the institution of marriage is failing, what or who is to blame, as well as what can or should be done to stop the breakdown of marriage in North America (Westbrook, 2010: 4). These are very important issues that do not only affect society in the United States but the world over, including Canada. Capagivism contributes in no small way to the vexing problem, and more specifically to 'the total number of out-of-wedlock births [which] is steadily rising. 'Capagivism is "the strategy of 'giving Canadian papers' [to someone else] through marriage [with him or her, most often being just business, not marriage per se]" (Fossungu, 2014a: 122). If they like the concept and are willing to learn for once from Canada and Africa, Americans can replace it with *Amepagivism*, and Australians with *Ausipagivism*, etc.

There will be two sets of victims/clients here, namely, (1) the Nigerian (Naja-Man) whose case was not actually and openly capagivistic in nature, and (2) the Cameroonians who all eyed and/or used capagivism. To aid you appreciate the Nigerian's stance in this troubling matter that even sex or *missoundi* could not divert, it is essential that you hear the *toto* definition(s) at length. *Toto* that Naja-man uses would be approximated to *missoundi* in Kirundi that is spoken in both Burundi and Rwanda, being also synonym to *mbombo* in Cameroon's Kamtok or Pidgin or Njangawatok. There is even this quip there about a very funny 'between-the-legs' match between *Mbombo* Njoya (a one-time Biya minister, now Sultan

34

of the Bamoun) and *Toto* Guillaume (a popular Cameroonian Makossa musician). *Mbombo* in the Bangwa language means the highway. Oh, how these languages relate to tell the full sex-slaving story! Some men obviously think *toto* is their highway to bliss. But they are noticeably forgetting some important catchy details, as reflected in the scholizyvettist capagivist's question to Momany in Fossungu (2014a: 123): "Are all African men as intelligent as you?" I will like you to get additional material for your response, as well as deepen your understanding of Nfon's *Greener from a Distance*(2013),[7] from Naja-man's and some Cameroonians' paper-getting adventures with the capagivists.

The *Toto* Story of Naja-man and the Québécoise

This is one hot tale of an African I met at Frito-Lays, a potato chips manufacturer in Pointe-Claire. Just arriving to town and knowing practically no one, this young and handsome Nigerian went to the popular Club Balatou (on 4372 Boulevard Saint-Laurent), a notorious spot where old white ladies and others usually pick up their young African potential capagivist victims/clients. From a home party that was abruptly stopped by the LaSalle police, a Guinean lady (with whom I had been chatting during the event) took me to Club Balatou, pretending it was also a first voyage of discovery for her. As soon as we got in, the lie lost its clothing. It is funny how liars don't just think straight. But is that not what defines them as liars? You will shortly hear the Guinean men calling her 'our sister'. "*Notre soeur*", *oui*: when all you hear about Guinean politics is that so-so-and-so is *Susu*, while this and that is *Malenké*! Moreover, if they think other Africans do not know what they mean by 'my sister/brother', then this particular African talking to you knows that only too well (see Fossungu, 2014b: 43-64). That is not the point here though. It is the way the Club Balatou regulars instantly know any newcomer.

---

[7]See http://www. langaa-rpcig. net/Greener-from-a-Distance. html.

Despite being conspicuously accompanied, the *Competition for Kumba* began as soon as I showed up. Every lady was requesting a dance while the Guinean and other African guys from Rossy Inc. were amazed to see me there. Back at Rossy Inc. the following Monday, the Guineans particularly wanted to know how I managed to "know" their sister. I just laughed and walked past these pretending Muslims, knowing of course that Naja-man had been easily grabbed by this working-class Quebec lady who merely needed him as her powerful 'Duracell-like' Black sex-machine.

She imposed her terms, as noted earlier in chapter 1. On her return from work she would bring along some alcoholic stuff to fortify the African machine. Sometimes she brings some cigarettes too. He would hastily eat and drink and smoke and then get to work, on her – the home factory. Naja-man was evidently losing patience with this routine but kept his patience. Unlike other Africans, Nigerians usually don't come out here to wallow around. They have focus and a well-defined plan that has to be carried out, one way or another. Unlike others (notably some of us from Cameroon who had to be rescued by a third-party – see Fossungu, 2014b: 49-50), Naja-man made it out on his own terms and as fast as possible. That is why he was there at Frito-Lay working and not idling at that lady's home waiting to work extremely hard only when she returns from work; eating and drinking just whatever she decides for him to eat or drink. There is a captivating inverse link here with Collins, who told me that it is the women in Botswana that are hardworking and look after the lazy, parasitic men who do nothing but eat and drink from the former's toil; largely explaining why Botswana women go crazy to have hardworking Zimbabwean men like him.

After listening to Naja-man to the end, some of my Francophone African friends could not hide their amazement that this guy was that *foolish* to have found *le paradis* that they are only dreaming of and then jumped out of it to come and be suffering in the factory *avec nous autres*. Naja-man was as well surprised at their reaction, letting them know they were just as brainless as "*Dat oyibo wey e think sey I leaf Naja come here only for sika toto. Which kanna toto wey I want weh no dey for Naja?*" (It is very silly for both you and the white woman to think that I came all the way from Nigeria just to be having sex in Canada. If that were the case, then I could have stayed back and had all the sex I could ever want right there in Nigeria, and very high quality women too.) At this point I was wishing I were Nigerian. But wait a minute! How unintelligent to be wishing to be what you are already! Aren't French-speaking Cameroonians defining the English-speaking there as *les Biafrans*?

All I could then say to the Nigerian was: "*Ma broda, your focus strong soteh e pass the one for dat American car wey them call sey Ford Focus.*" But then I began wondering again if Ford *Focuses* on anything than *Exploring* how to *Fuse* Japanese designs and *Escape* being *Edged* in by their *Escort* for *Fiesting* around with *Taurusing* and *Flexing Mustang*. Like Nigeria also does all the time with car designs, Naja-man obviously did not use *ben-ben* methods like Ford to edge himself out of the sex-slaving cage of the Québécoise. He was direct and to the point because he owns himself. Naja-man's focus is not only impressive; it is also natural, if you judge by the standard of some of us coming from French-speaking Africa. Never mind the camouflage indicating that Cameroon is also Anglophone. Bullshit. Some of us just stay Anglophone there because we were born to be and stay authentic even in the midst of all the artificiality and imitations. But just hear me in Nigeria, for instance. I am worrying about how to communicate with my people in Cameroon since I don't yet have a P. O. Box or PMB at the post office. "*Abi, na where you come from?*" That is the landlord wondering. "Just use the address of your apartment *shah*." Amazed or dazzled, you choose which of them you think better captures my reaction when the man gave me the full address. Yes, most Africans get here before learning a lot of things that the Nigerian has known for ages, arriving here with a clear goal in mind. How less focused can someone like that be? Is that not the reason Nigerians are hardly liked by the West? And how come their Cameroonian neighbours are not even emulating them?

Cameroonians and the Capagivists

There are countless cases but we will survey just three of these Anglophone capagivistic matches, two from Savannazone and one from Debundschazone: Bali-man versus Capa-Canada; Amumba-man versus Capa-Mali; and 99-senser versus Capa-Haiti.

Bali-man versus Capa-Canada

This is the account of a Savannazone guy of the Bali ethnic group. On his arrival in Montreal from Europe, this very hardworking young, well-built and tall man also met his white girlfriend (Capa-Canada) in a club in downtown. They left the club that night and went to the lady's apartment where they thereafter began living together, enjoying practically all the rights and obligations of what is known in Cameroon as '*came we stay*' (common law spouses). Bali-man was really in love with the woman and seriously thinking of settling down with her, for better and for worse. I say this because an African man (or woman) would not be appearing in all community events with a partner unless that intention is there. Such public appearances are some kinds of hindrances to any further acquaintances. But Bali-man's did not just end there. The *chop mob* or hard core kissing in public during said events would speak volumes of their own. Any Cameroonian lady that might have been nursing or harbouring hopes of getting Bali-man's attention simply gave up because, as they put it, Bali-man "*don really go alanu. Dis kanna public chop mob so e don pass mark*" (he has clearly reached the land of no-return).

In the meantime Bali-man's case with the IRB (Immigration and Refugee Board) was not looking good at all. He was initially not panicking since he was looking forward to and even requesting marriage with his darling. Capa-Canada kept playing 'wait-and-see' while getting her sex job done and done and done. Can what these two lovers were confronting be tied to the christickinological theory or advice of "Don't start living as husband and wife until you are husband and wife" (Fossungu, 2014a: 110) or to something else? The guy was still there hoping against hope that capagivism would turn the tide. It seems as if Capa-Canada had no intention to settle with the guy but just to have him as her sex machine. This guy who loved the woman and was contributing more than fully to the household just could not comprehend the woman he thought loved him as well. Panic, panic, panic, was then all over the place for him. But just see how nature turns the tide sometimes. Bali-man was eventually accepted as a convention refugee! It was then the scheming foolish lady's turn to press for the marriage that she had been putting off. The man had already seen clearly what that would mean (and was in store) and off he immediately went with: "*Dat ngah tinsey I be whetty? E mami pimma ya!*" (What does that woman take me for? That I am a big fool, right? To hell with her!) If Bali-man turned out not to be *mbombo*-idiotic, another Savannazonian (or North-Westerner) seems to have been one *toto*-fool.

Amumba-Man versus Capa-Mali

Amumba-man was studying medicine at the Université de Montréal and needed to become a permanent resident. Due to the Canadian immigration roundabout exclusion directed at foreign students (see chapter 3), he contacted Capa-Mali who was willing to give him the status through the capagivistic procedures of payment, marriage and sponsorship. It was strictly to be business – cash for the deal of marriage and sponsorship. Consensual divorce to follow after Amumba-man has become a permanent resident. But somewhere along the line Capa-Mali seemed to have cooked up other plans. She asked the man to actually move in with her 'in order to have the show believable'. That was unsuspiciously done by Amumba-man who was badly in need of the "papers" and status to be able to evolve with 'borderlessness' in Canada and the USA. Already living in her apartment, (irresistible) sex, of course, followed and, no doubt, you can scarcely avoid impregnating a woman (you regularly climb on) if that is her desire. The baby-trap was thus very easy in materializing. Oh Scholizyvettism!

With that *toto*-loving error Amumba-man was into slavery forever, one way or another. After all, are they not also legally and officially married? It was too late to turn back at that point. Capa-Mali already had both the knife and yam. It is not necessary for me to delve into the man's frustration resulting from the scholizyvettist pregnancy trap. The plain fact is that, with or without divorce, Amumba-man is the woman's slave for life – either child support calculated on a medical doctor's salary or staying around and doing Capa-Mali's bidding. Seeing just how costly the first option was, Amumba-man had to give up his lucrative appointment at Harvard University and return to Montreal for the second, what the scheming lady is interested in, in the first place.

In all of this the greatest loser is the child who will grow up not knowing and feeling the parental affection that every child deserves to have. It is only certain that a mother who uses pregnancy in this scholizyvettist manner can hardly be said to love the issue of that pregnancy (see Fossungu, 2014a: 83-85). Similarly, a father that has been tricked as such into parenthood could scarcely love (no matter how much he tries) the child or the trapping device that he would most often, if not always, see as the cause of his enslavement. Yes. This is a whole separate ball game from the case of Momany in several respects. First, Momany has "some inborn powers" that not everyone has (Fossungu, 2013a: vii). These natural gifts do enable him to see the child in this particular case exactly as he/she is – a victim too. Second, in his proper situation Momany was never successfully trapped into marriage, even as pregnancy/children would later be employed by the other parent to attain certain illicit goals (see more in part two below). Like Momany, another Bangwa man also skilfully dodged the sex-and-pregnancy trap of capagivists.

99-Senser versus Capa-Haiti

A fool of any kind comes nowhere close to 99-senser. Perhaps these Bangwa people are not styled 99-sensers by Cameroonians for nothing? The case of this Bangwa man is quite 99-sensically interesting.[8] A student then in Concordia University, 99-Senser (like most foreign students in Canada) wanted to be a permanent resident before graduating. He was already living with his girlfriend – to later be his wife. An excellent bonus, you would say. 99-Senser shopped around the capagivist circle (that he was very familiar with) until he found Capa-Haiti who was also living with her boyfriend. A Perfect Match! The temptation of cohabiting was eliminated, leaving the affair to be solely business 'from A to Z' or *alesji teh mee*, as the Bangwa say. The only actual hold-tight or *collé-collé* ever between these two business people was the very believable 'You can now kiss the bride' during the *officialising* ceremony. Being Bangwa, this writer was invited and present at the ceremony and can frankly tell you that Capa-Haiti was a real professional capagivist, judging from the fact that her Haitian boyfriend tactically was absent (in the hall) as the kissing act got near. Betraying jealousy was thus excluded one hundred percent.

---

8 For extensive discussion of the 99-Sense Theory, see Fossungu, 2014a.

41

Already a permanent resident, the only issue with 99-Senser had to do with how to also *capagive* in regard of his Cameroonian girlfriend or wife-to-be who was also a student at the Université de Montréal. He could not, of course, have been the capagivist since he was legally married to Capa-Haiti until the divorce decree. Being the Canada-savvy guy that he is, he went into another capagivistic contract for the girlfriend, this time the gear-lever being a Cameroonian man he knew. These Africans who do not usually stick to their word! *Na ben-ben man wey e bi finnam dis time mo-oh!* The girlfriend's own capagivism thus fell apart along the way because the male capagivist wanted the 'corner-corner' *mbombo* thing, as clearly exhibited in his comportment that was anything but upfront. When it comes to seriousness in marriage and family in Cameroon, Bameleke women could compete only with *Amumba* (Savannazonian) women for the first position. I am sure the *ben-ben* guy made away with the half payment since the stunned Bameleke lady was not willing (thanks also to her cohabiting with 99-Senser) to play the *'cunny-man'* game. She quickly changed gear to something else – leaving *foreign-student-unfriendly* Canada for good for the *open-competition* USA where everything quickly worked out just fine for her. She and her husband are now very successful American citizens, whereas Canada would have surely frustrated them or long sent these brilliant and resourceful foreign students packing for the gaol called Cameroon.

On Capa-Haiti's part, the most important worry (as reported by 99-Senser himself) was that of not *falling choki*. That is one real huge risk that money-crazy capagivists take, with some of them sometimes so hastily after the thousands-of-dollar contract price (and ulterior *toto* or *mblacaus* enjoyment) that they do not stop to think about. Would the client stay clear of welfare money during the three-year period (for spouses)? Yes, the risk is real. Should he/she get into welfare during said duration it is the capagivist-sponsor that reimburses the totality of sums collected to the Welfare Department, as per the undertaking pact signed with the Quebec Government (for those in this province) or the Federal Government for those in the other provinces and territories. 99-Senser had then reassured Capa-Haiti that there was no need to worry about that since "I am not the type that would even consider for a minute this demeaning thing called welfare. How can that ever permit a hardworking, many-responsibilities person like me to accomplish what I am looking for 'the papers' to be able to do?" Both parties therefore ended up happy with each other, having stayed true to the agreement – the outcome of positive competition and self-help. They both thus avoided giving each other any ground for feeling as or passing for a victim.

The Silliest Creation of a Victim in Canada?

You can then see that both Naja-man and 99-Senser (especially in regard of the girlfriend) took control of their lives and made the bold decision not to enslave themselves through SEX simply because of "Canadian Papers", documents and status that may not even begin to be the solution to their problems. Collins didn't even find himself in this category (or, could he be the wife's sponsor and under threats of her getting into welfare if…?). Yet, unlike Bali-man, he accepted being and remaining a slave for sex. It is truly a pity that someone can do this to himself! Is Collins really a victim here or what? We shall find out with two heads: (1) the marriage's MSF strategy and (2) a liar who does not keep word.

The Collinsian Marriage's 'Médicins-Sans-Frontières' Strategy

Like globalization's dubious concept of deterritorialization (or 'End-of-the-Nation-State'), would St. Prisoner Collins and his 'partner' not just then be employing the concept of 'marriage' simply to attain the same objectives as those of

Médicins Sans Frontières (MSF)? The English version says 'Doctors without Borders' but I am wondering whether the most appropriate translated description (for *médicins sans frontières*) should not instead be 'borderless doctors'. Debrix (1998) makes the MSF – Doctors without Borders – the case study in his examination of the phenomenon of international medical assistance to populations in distress. He does so from the perspective of the new spatial strategies deployed by medical humanitarian organizations, showing how 'members' of MSF actually move across and within national borders without restrictions that would normally apply to non-members of the group. In this sense, Debrix thinks the "MSF can be read as a War Machine" that "challenges the territorial authority of State apparatuses" (1998: 831). This feature of the organization, it is said, is necessitated by the very *humanitarian* nature of its members' job – that of being able to help those in areas of the world affected by natural disasters, wars, or other calamities, and in dire need of critical medical assistance. This ideology sounds very much to me like Thomas Friedman's suggestion that, like colonialism, "the free market of globalization also needs a 'hidden fist'" (Sparke, 2013: 40). Just how free then is free market? And how borderless are MSF's activities?

Debrix answers by theorizing that the "MSF's brand of medical humanitarianism is…[just] as much a matter of *reterritorialisation* as it is a question of *deterritorialisation*" (1998: 829-830, original emphasis). What happens here is that the MSF goes beyond state borders to create new territorial structures, one of which is the 'space of victimhood'. (Is Collins actually a victim?) Under the pretext of reaching victims all over the world, the MSF constructs new spaces called 'humanitarian zones' (that is the Collinsian marriage). Inside them, "individuals in distress are identified as 'victims', are sorted out, and become recognizable as generalized examples of human drama" (Debrix, 1998: 827). Does this not also sound like the barb-wired free trade zones? Could one also smell the hand of the military-industrial complex at work here? This complex refers to the unique 'one-percent' dictatorship that President Dwight Eisenhower warned Americans about (see Fossungu, 2014b: 138-140 & 97-98 n.38). And, what is worse still, the MSF reterritorialization is blanketed in deception, making it "perhaps more dangerous, harmful and specious than the more traditional strategies of the state since it seeks to hide behind an appearance of deterritoriality and borderlessness" (Debrix, 1998: 839). Let's therefore stop calling the Collinsian thing 'marriage' when in actual fact it is voluntary 'sex-slaving'.

On N'a Pas Le Choix: Trying to explain what François Debrix means in the last passage would also bring to light another nagging problem with the MSF (as well as Collins' potential claim to *je n'ai pas le choix*). The MSF claims 'neutrality'. But after lengthily examining that concept Debrix discovered that neutrality here, in effect, is productive of space (1998: 834-835). This is a very harmful type of space production because it is camouflaged. As Paasi has counselled, "[t]erritoriality is also embedded in the daily lives of citizens in the forms of personal relations and property relationships. Boundedness and territory are thus important *processes* embedded in the production and reproduction of social relations on various scales, i. e. they have to be studied critically rather than assuming or declaring them in normative terms to be *passés*" (Paasi, 2009: 215, original emphasis). 'One Has No Choice' (*On n'a pas le choix*) is a very familiar phrase that Africans generally employ to cloak the fact that they have chosen not to stand up for their rights. We always have a choice between defending our rights and not defending them. Saying there is no choice is just an escapist way of shying away from doing the normal thing. And that is where the dictator or oppressor smiles.

This discussion is also important to understanding the stereotyping of Africa in America because rather than perform its traditional role of helping to educate the public and being the watch-dog of society, the American media has become the mouthpiece for neoliberal commodification that Sparke (2013: 57-95) has lengthily discussed. But Debrix (1998: 843) cautions that the blame for the "commodification of humanitarianism" here is not that of the media, it is rather that of international medical assistance specialists who "intervene across and beyond borders to find new territorial arrangements, new lands and new subjects to place inside these territories. " Thus, from this MSF example, contemporary medical humanitarianism "suggests that deterritorialisation may be its own territorial strategy, another geopolitical marking, a new spatial demarcation with its own regime of power and knowledge" (Debrix, 1998: 830). Yes, François Debrix, you really know what has been going on with these doctors who want us to think they are borderless. The reader has just seen our Université de Montréal 'doctor without border' (Amumba-man) realizing in the end that there was just too strong a Malian-erected border he could simply not defy: despite his being borderless in North America! Oh, just see what the alluring 'Highway to Borderlessness' called *Mbombo* can instead lead you to! My fellow men, you had each therefore better be disciplining your troublesome *mblacaus* or penis while I take an extensive look at a liar who doesn't keep her word, whether or not mbombo and mblacaus are involved.

A Liar Who Does Not Keep Word

Some people just do not think. I once wondered aloud to Flavie why the two children in Cameroon are bearing her family name rather than their father's. Her answer was that she changed their name because their father is *"un fenéant qui ne fait rien pour moi et les enfants"* (a good-for-nothing idiot who does

46

absolutely nothing for me and the children). My spontaneous reaction to her was: "So, if tomorrow we are no longer together, that's what you will also do?" It may be easier to do in lawless and disorderly Cameroon but, unfortunately for her, that is not something you easily do in Canada, as Schola can quickly testify. She too tried it but failed because I also have to sign any papers for such a change. Bravo Canada! Do these mothers actually consider what is best for the children? From Flavie's response, you can see clearly exactly why some of these women go about "shitting children", to borrow from Mami Regina Akiefac Fossungu (see Fossungu, 2013a: 12). These children, to them, are only good as instruments of blackmail, intimidation, and wealth acquisition (see Fossungu, 2014a: chapter 3).

Flavie's lawyer (Me. Patrice Gravel) actually told me in April 2014 through email (concerning my request for change of the April 2, 2014 date for the hearing) that she alone has had the children all this while anyway, which entitles her, *d'office*, to full custody of them. Of course, that is exactly the veiled strategy I am doing my best to clear up by (for instance) returning to school. I did it so that I could thereafter have a regular job which will permit me to be with them (including the others abroad that I have been trying to bring to Canada) all year round. There is a mountain of evidence to show that I have tried with becoming a lawyer (professional and academic) in Canada, to no avail. Although I have not given up on lawyering yet, I have left no stone unturned, explaining why I was then in Windsor pursuing an M. A. in Political Science. I am hoping that as a formal political scientist (that I have also always wanted to be – see Fossungu, 2013a: 54), fortified with my legal backyard, I would more easily be able to pin my feet firmly somewhere in Canada, be it in government, industry, or academia. I have also been trying my hand at just anything that can permit us bring up these children together in an ideal home – defined as one requiring "that both parents be there together

47

to bring up the children and advance the family" (Fossungu, 2013a: 117). But Flavie (who loves free-riding a lot) has been doing everything to ensure that I only remain working in the forest. In that way then she can easily take cover behind the fact that she has the children anyways, a ploy which also seems to be aimed at furthering her claim to victimhood.

Irrespective of our individual motives, Flavie and I had the *choice* to do what we voluntarily did to bring these two children into the world. But they, as any other child, do not have any choice in deciding who their parents are to be (see Fossungu, 2014a: 69-70); and, unless someone can boldly and truthfully stand up and speak out on their behalf, these children are completely helpless then as well. I wrote *Africans in Canada* "solely because of my concern for the future of children and social work departments that have enormous powers over the making or ruining of the future of children (whatever the definition [of child, biological or otherwise, that is] attached)" (Fossungu, 2013a: vii). For the victimhood pretension before Canadian Courts and other Institutions, I will be speaking here from the point of the women because that is where I have my own personal experience, a substantial part of which I have already shared with the entire world. But the women are not alone because I also know several cases of the men on the other side of the 'victimhood game'. Just imagine this admirable Cameroonian lady who worked her ass to death and sponsored her husband to join her in Montreal. There was a splendid reception party organized to welcome the ungrateful idiot who, at the same party, was very disgracefully jumping at the wife's female friends! As Cameroon's Prince Ndedy Eyango sings, *'Between man and woman no put your mob'*; we may then not know exactly what is between the two (justifying also my relying more on my case whose full facts I know). But whatever it may be, the man's comportment is truly pathetic. Could his intention here not be to have the wife heatedly kick him out so that he could then further screw her life up by getting into social welfare? Otherwise, how else could one convincingly explicate this man's strange behaviour? Dear Hardworking Wife *plus* Cheap Victimhood-crazy Husband?

I would like to capitalize on this victimhood topic here because that is obviously the picture Flavie wants to hang before the eyes of the Court (and other institutions of this country). The design is to mislead it (them) into falling for her free-riding schemes. I surely know what I am talking about, and also know that it is not just the case that was before the Quebec Court (and still somewhat *pending* –since the May 2014 order was only provisional) that needs to provoke a rethinking in the way Family Courts do business in this country. I believe that you would better comprehend the present situation in the Quebec institution mostly through understanding the one also put up in 2005-2006 by Flavie's *predecessor* – thanks very much to Ontario's London Family High Court. Flavie is out to sort of foolishly *copycat* Schola, someone she was supposed to be indefinitely replacing.

Very briefly put, Schola also claimed persecution in Cameroon consequent on my critical thinking, as expressed in newspaper writings there. It is kind of odd, but I do not (and did not) doubt her: viewing what was going on there and my 1998 views (see Fossungu, 2014b: 89-91). The more especially too in view of my more recent detailed expositions in *Democracy and Human Rights in Africa* (Fossungu, 2013c). My belief and awareness of Schola's critical situation in Cameroon would explain why (rather than stop expressing my views) I did everything I could to get her out of there and into Canada, where she was given refuge (File Number M99-02879). As soon as Schola was in, a lot of doubts set in. Because she then refused to sponsor me to also get into Canada, on the basis that "I know the day you will have papers you will run" (Fossungu, 2014a: 78). As noted, this style of Take and Take and Take (or *99-Sensism*) is already extensively examined in both *Africans in Canada* (Fossungu, 2013a) and *Africa's*

Anthropological Dictionary on Love and Understanding (Fossungu, 2014a), with the latter book graphically exposing the blatant use of 'Children, Pregnancies, and Abortions' by some women right here in Canada as potent tools for "screwing up" not only their so-called spouses/partners, but also (above all else) the 'children'.

A few questions will suffice here to wiggle your mind. What was Schola making of her husband's own safety in Cameroon too? Was her claim of persecution there because of the husband's critical writings true or false victimhood? Was she really coming to Canada as someone's spouse or just using that spouse *status* as a bridge to get here to *only* realize the schemes they (she and her parents) had cooked up back there: at the expense of the children and supposed spouse? More of the puzzling scholaparentist questions could be pursued in aforementioned books. But my stressed point here is that Canadians generally and the authorities in particular must learn to understand this confusion, especially from most of the Africans that come here and scathingly misemploy concepts that Canadians commonly grasp differently. For instance, 'my children' that means just that to Canadians, to them instead would mean, in fact, 'my money-getting apparatuses', 'my means of intimidation', etc. ; Capa-Mali's case already noted above being strong proof.

Flavie is out to deliberately confuse the Court (and other institutions) into taking me for an unfit parent/partner. And this is designed for her easy swim into her world of compulsive free-riding; and this time, not just riding on me but also on Canada, simultaneously. And, as I have said, the family courts of this country have (unknowingly?) proven to be perfect tools in the hands of women like this. It is about time these courts wake up and stop assisting fake victims to endlessly continue to ruin the *avenir* of innocent children. When a mother, for instance, is bent on destroying or limiting the partner's chances of progress (solely for her own petty agenda), does she ever

50

realize exactly what she is doing to the children that she is claiming to love, and entitled to full custody of them? Does a mother also have the child at all in mind when she argues unnecessary with the child's day-care provider?

Filomena Pima Gonzalez will better tell you more on Flavie's current and on-going case while I handle Schola's. A Nigerian lady was operating a home day-care in LaSalle. It is there that we found a place for our daughter. The rules were clear enough. For example, lateness in picking up children was paid for by the minute. I was known in Rossy Inc. to always *punch out* thirty minutes before closing time in order to beat the traffic congestion on the Decarie Expressway (AutoRoute 15 South). I always got to the day-care on time. But not on the day in question when we arrived together there about ten minutes late due to Schola's fault. The day-care provider very politely stated the fine and Schola's war immediately began. She was not paying anything for *just* ten minutes lateness. The argument became so heated and insolent. I intervened and told Schola to stop what she was doing and just pay the penalty because we were late and the rules were simple enough. She turned on me aggressively, telling me to be sure to pack when we get home and join the woman I was supporting. I told her right there that I didn't need her "to tell me to go after the lady, if that is actually what I want to do; because I see her every day, morning and evening." It is amazing how some of these people think. That because you are married to them you must take their side even when they are dead wrong! Could someone remind them that I am not another Collins, because I know that marriage is not the synonym for slavery, please? But that apart, how could a parent gratuitously pick a fight with someone who looks after his/her child from morning to evening? Does such a parent really love said child?

I sometimes just cannot help weeping when (on the very few occasions I even have to be with them) my son in London always keeps calling me 'Uncle. . .' before correcting to

51

'Daddy'. As you can see, *Daddy* is almost out of his vocabulary, since he is always surrounded only by uncles and aunts (his mother's siblings). In August 2014, the day-care provider (Filomena) for the ones in Montreal (Peter and Peteraf) left a message on my answering machine that did the same thing to me. Three-year old Peteraf came in that day and would not let her or anyone else there have peace with the demand to talk to his father. Where is he and is he coming soon? Filomena therefore wanted me to call as usual (as I do when I am in Windsor) to talk to them while they were at day-care. But how could I possibly do that when I am locked in the forest all day and return to the camp only after they must have left day-care? That is the result of Schola's redefinition of family in Canada to exclude 'children' and 'spouse', but nevertheless using these same non-family-member "tools" to legalize her schemes through the unsuspecting and very willing Canadian Family Courts. Amazing!

I wonder if that is not precisely what Flavie also wants to use the Court to achieve. Were it otherwise, why would she be hiding her address and whereabouts when she ran away with our two children on January 24, 2013? And worse still, doing so on a day that I (who drive) did not take them to day-care because of extremely cold weather. And her lawyer joyfully told me then that she was entitled not to have me know where she was putting up with the children. (Of course, the lawyer too is in her darkness, I must assume). You do not need to go too far to get the clouds with which my name and honour are being clothed in, when you simply couple the picture created here with Flavie's *Affidavit Circonstancié* of January 30, 2013 which states: *". . . 23. Monsieur est venu à plusieurs réprises au petit matin en état d'ébriété avancé. Il a même une fois été malade de boisson dans sa voiture au mois de novembre 2012"*. Note, in addition, that I (who had been living with and solely providing for her since 2009, and having two children with her) do not have a name at all in

2012, just Monsieur. 2012 is quite a significant year for this relationship indeed.

Of course, the calculated full intention here needs no rocket scientist to glean. Hyphenating the created events of the previous paragraph with my being a Canadian citizen and her situation still hanging in the air, clearly puts into the mind of anyone who is without the untwisted facts that Peter Ateh-Afac Fossungu (Sr.) is not only a drunkard, but also someone who abuses both his children and partner. Perfecto, you would say? She and her cohorts must have convinced themselves that this strategy provides her with a sure door to free-riding on Canadians, under the pretext of being a battered victim. Liars just don't think straight, they always *forget* some important details that then hit back like a boomerang. Not only is it that the fabricated portrait is someone else's, not mine; but also that courts don't usually make decisions based on one side of the story, except the other side (that has been duly served) chooses not to present its own version and supporting facts. Canadian Courts must be intelligent enough not to fall for Flavie's cheap shots, especially after some light is made to shine on the darkness that she and her *uninformed* advisers have mounted.

For a start, I wonder if I even looked like a drunkard to any reasonable person in the courtroom. Or, let's assume that anyone is silly enough not to be able to tell that in court, perhaps, because I might have *sobered-up* for the purpose of the appearance. Then, of course, that means that I am always sober. Otherwise, my immediate community would be even sillier to be honouring a drunken societal outfit for outstanding community service, exemplary leadership, *qualité exceptionnelle de son travail*, etc., as the Cameroon Goodwill Association of Montreal (CGAM) and others like the Université de Montréal have done (see Fossungu, 2013a: 110). Quite apart from other strings of testimonies, I guess that only an exceptional perpetual drunkard can be able to (1) obtain the academic qualifications I have (see Fossungu, 2013a: 53-54) and (2) publish three books in one year (see Fossungu, 2013a-c). Or, maybe– just maybe – both Schola and Flavie have been the *real things* that have been keeping me so *drunken* that I could not have written a thing while they were in my blood stream and perturbing my head. Else, it is not clear how we are to explicate the fact that, from 1996, I was producing at least one academic journal article every year until 1999 when Schola got to Canada[9]: with my next article thereafter only appearing in 2010. [10] 2010 is like Flavie's own 1999. I must say I have to say what I have to say just to show you the kind of scheming liar we are dealing with here, the sponsorships and her own scholadela assumption providing the way forward.

The Sponsorships and Scholadela Assumption

The concept of *scholadela assumption* (Fossungu, 2014a: 120-124), very simply put, describes situations like that of Bali-man, with Capa-Canada assuming that he is in a position of 'what-

---

[9]See Peter Ateh-Afac Fossungu: "999 University, Please Help the Third World (Africa) Help Itself: A Critique of Council Elections" 64 *Journal of Air Law and Commerce* (1999), 339-375; "Parliamentary, Congressional and Advanced Governments in Comparative Perspectives: The Unbridgeable Gulfs" 37 *Juridis Info (Revue de Législation et de Jurisprudence Camerounaises)* (1999), 74-76; "The ICAO Assembly: The Most Unsupreme of Supreme Organs in the United Nations System? A Critical Analysis of Assembly Sessions" 26 *Transportation Law Journal* (1998), 1-49; "Federalism as A Guarantee to Judicial Independence and Fundamental Human Rights: Reflecting on 'Political Intellectualism' in Cameroon and Laying the Ghost of the 'Federal' Republique du Cameroun to Rest" 33 *Juridis Info (Revue de Législation et de Jurisprudence Camerounaises)* (1998), 56; "Sentencing Criminals in Cameroon: Tying Judges' Hands and Expecting Them to Do Gymnastics?" 29 *Juridis Périodique (Revue de Droit et de Science Politique)* (1997), 84–98; and "Cameroon Sentencing Law: Let's Talk 'Diminished Responsibility'" 25 *Juridis Périodique (Revue de Droit et de Science Politique)* (1996), 84–89.

[10]See Peter Ateh-Afac Fossungu, "Separation of Powers in Public International Law: Is the International Civil Aviation Organization (ICAO) Out of or Within the United Nations System? A Critique of ICAO Assembly Elections" 35 *Annals of Air & Space Law* (2010), 267-296.

54

else-can-he-do than do my bidding?' Flavie is and always will be the mother of our children. But that fact does not of itself provide any excuse for a spade not to be called a spade. We are where we are today solely because Flavie is a blatant liar who does not care one bit about keeping her word. If Flavie was actually the one paying him, I am very sure Me. Gravel would have been in a nice position to quickly confirm this thesis. Too bad that she has never learnt how to spend money that she has normally worked hard for. That makes it even more extremely important that Canadian Institutions should help her to obtain such invaluable life instruction. Before I later get into some *documented* details that support that thesis, you could get the tip of the iceberg of confirmation from some other sources, including these two people particularly: Filomena Pina Gonzales (the day-care provider for our two children) and Derick Yegha Duma. In 2010 Derick supplied Flavie with perfumes worth hundreds of dollars on the exceptional understanding (because of me) that he would be paid after Flavie has sold the products. As we converse today in November 2014, Derick has never received his money or the unsold perfumes. And I am of course to eventually repay him because, but for my sake, he would never have made that exception of delivering to her without upfront payment of the purchase price.

If your spouse or partner can lie to you about his/her children that he/she had before ever meeting you, on what else would such a person not lie about? And if you are truly the drunkard and abusive person that you are painted as being, would you (after discovering this big lie and several others) still go ahead and seek to ameliorate things for both liar and said children? But that is what this 'drunkard and abusive person' talking to you has endlessly tried to do. I know many people would be wondering here: "What on earth was he thinking doing that?" The answer is very simple, if you get to know who exactly I am, especially from reading not only *Africans in Canada*

55

but also *Africa's Anthropological Dictionary on Love and Understanding*. You will then know that I am someone who is devoted to 'bettering the lives of the greatest number of persons possible'. That being the case, you would then see why it is wholly illogical to exclude from that 'greatest number of persons possible' someone I intend to spend the rest of my life with.

I met Flavie in Montreal in early January 2009 at a Cameroonian event. We *traditionally married* in May 2009. I do not usually get into doing anything unless I intend doing it, and doing it well. With Flavie, the ceremony was traditional merely because my legal divorce with Schola was then not yet final, becoming so only in October 2012. This 2012! Official or not, I have posited already that marriage is more in what/how the parties to it feel, not simply the piece of paper evidencing it. It is a commitment to each other. That is clearly my take on marriage and family. Let me note that there is a lot to take you back to in view of the commencement of my effort to positively change the lives of Flavie and the two children in Douala, Cameroon. Biological to me or not, I consider them as my children. It may pay to note here that the parents that raised me are indeed not my biological parents (see Fossungu, 2013a: 4-11).

As noted in chapter 4 of *Africa's Anthropological Dictionary on Love and Understanding*, the first sponsorship for them failed to materialize because of arrears of child support to Schola, arrears that had accrued during the several months I was unable to pay, being out of work through Schola's doings (see Fossungu, 2013a: 84-86). Thus, a letter dated 20 Avril, 2011 was addressed to Flavie from the Embassy of Canada in Dakar, Senegal, stating in bold print that *"Votre répondant PETER FOSSUNGU ne s'est pas qualifié et a été refusé par le Ministère de l'Immigration et des Communautés Culturelles du Québec. Il serait donc contraire à la Réglementation de vous émettre un visa de résident permanent. Votre demande est donc rejetée."* Before this letter, I had already received a letter to the same effect in 2010 from the Quebec Government based on *"le paiement **d'une pension alimentaire** à votre épouse...."* In late 2010, I again undertook to sponsor the trio as well as Tsopzem Kelie Fossungu, my first daughter who is still in Cameroon as I speak. Kelie's case is another sad instance of some women not being able to look beyond their noses. I am not getting deep into that here: except to indicate to you that I am bent on doing everything in my powers to unite all these children, full or half siblings. I simply do not want any of them to ever live through what I have myself experienced, such as only knowing that I had half siblings when I was thirty-four! That is one of the forces driving my concern and responsibility to Lindsey Hervée, Kelie, and Scott Alexandre – blood sisters and brother to Peter, Jr. , and Peteraf, the latter two also being blood brothers to the two in London, Ngunyi and Nguajong – all four in Canada (a girl and three boys) being born in Quebec. It was thus not so much about Flavie as it was for these children that I was doing the sponsorships.

But for all their sponsorships to happen, I had to have eliminated every dime in the arrears of child support to Schola that was still pending. I Looked at the larger picture as I always do (I am wondering if this is something you would rightly attribute to a drunkard and abusive person). On doing so, I realized that the elimination of the arrears would take such a long time (if not forever) and the only way through was to have Schola withdraw the issue from the Family Responsibility Office (FRO) and I pay the sum (as per monthly arrangement) directly to her, while doing other necessary things such as freely travelling around and the sponsorships. Until this time I could not even travel to the USA, let alone to teach at the Université de Douala where I had been engaged. I am not quite sure that the Ontario institutions treated me at all fairly in this matter. First, they rushed to act on whatever lies Schola had fabricated without considering her free-riding schemes that I was warning them about. But that is 'Yours to Discover' Ontario, different, no doubt, from 'Je Me Souviens' Quebec. There is no need for me to get into all the missed job opportunities down there in the USA and elsewhere because of this unwise issue of suspending the passport of a job seeker, from whom you are demanding money.

Second, was it actually necessary for my life to be pointlessly put on hold for close to six years? Just imagine your spouse leaving your in September 2004 and then suing for divorce and all its accompanying child this and child that in July 2006. There is then an Endorsement by Justice Henry Vogelsang dated March 20, 2007 and which clearly stated that "[1] This brief divorce trial featured little real contest. The only apparent dispute between the parties involved their differing views about the reason for their separation and who ought to be saddled with fault for it...." Yet, you are only legally divorced from her/him "31 days after the date of this order [of October 2, 2012." Isn't that really amazing? Did the London Court really need those amounts of years to issue the divorce order? The incredulity here is even magnified when you realize that between the two dates given above all you get in response to your numerous enquiries to the court regarding the divorce order is that you need to get a lawyer to represent you on the matter! Why on earth do I need a lawyer just to know that, when the case was heard and the decision taken on it while I was representing myself? Are these some of the kinds of things included in the Ontario Bar's claims that I do not know their law enough, perhaps? Mechanical Law indeed![11] Could I be

---

[11] Professor Donald Smiley, tell them more on the issue, please. "As a non-lawyer, it seems clear to me that if Canadian courts are to assume a more active role in the ranking and defining of human rights there must be profound changes in the Canadian legal culture [because] Canadian jurists are profoundly [still] in the positivist tradition. But the determination of human rights in particular circumstances is in Peter Russell's terms the 'delicate balancing of social priorities'" (Smiley, 1992: 463).

correct in thinking that it is just 'Yours to Discover' Ontario, and that it is different from 'Je Me Souviens' Quebec? I wouldn't even need to bother you with indicating that the Ontario Mechanical Court applied its Ontario 'law' without in the least bothering about 'private international law' principles whereas not everyone involved in the case (plaintiff, defendant, and children) was resident in Ontario/Ontarian. Remember too that said children are born in Quebec. Would the Nigerian filmmakers be wrong then in calling some of these Canadian lawyers 'charge and bail lawyers'? Anyways, all that was caused by Flavie's predecessor, but it is difficult to argue that this is not what she too is now after.

Whatever the case (as already mentioned in Fossungu, 2014a: 132-134), with Flavie's full knowledge, in November-December 2010, I made several trips to London, Ontario, to negotiate the withdrawal deal with Schola. By March 2011, the file was no longer with the FRO. (Thank you very much, Schola.) I then put in the sponsorship applications of Flavie and the children again. I did so after having made it clear to Flavie that its success depended largely on my respecting the agreement with Schola particularly, stressing that the most important thing at the time was for Flavie and the said children to become landed in Canada. That this entailed that she had to put in extra efforts in diminishing her regressive comportment or nonoselfism and also in seeing to it that both of us work hand in hand so that I can be able to keep to my engagement to all the parties, including Flavie herself. Frankly, would there even be need for such preaching to anyone who has the genuine interests of his/her children at heart? Wasn't this just the kind of partner any sensible person would be praying to God every day to let him/her have?

But Flavie behaved all along as if my multiple engagements had absolutely nothing to do with her. She even was very silly to consider it a *fait accompli* (her own scholadela assumption) by instead heightening the exhibition of the comportment that unmistakably indicated that, as soon as the trio were effectively landed in Canada, she was ready to push me deep down into another bottomless hole rather than aiding me to come out of the Schola endless crack. Her attitude explains why we are even having said court case, a suit that she is manifestly using to paint herself as a victim; an obvious abuse of concepts. Canadian Courts must make a clear distinction between a *real victim* and a *self-made* or *camouflaged victim* (see Fossungu, 2014b: 212-214). The proof so far overwhelmingly shows that, if she is a victim at all (which she is not), Flavie belongs to the latter, which must then drag in something similar to the *ex turpi causa non oritur actio* doctrine. I will document a few more cases that led to a sort of classic case of divine intervention that my humble life is chockfull of.

Take, first, her comportment at the hospital in November 2011 when Peteraf was born. I filled the hospital forms as had long been mutually agreed. But Flavie listens only to the people who are out there conducting her. After I had signed and handed the forms to her to also sign, she cancelled information on it, putting in whatever some friend of hers in France had recently told her to, before signing. I would not want to describe here the scene she then created at the maternity, simply because I inquired if she understood the consequences of cancelling things on the form with my signature already on it. Pius Esambe Etube, who signed that same form as witness (as well as his wife, Florence Ahone Etube who was also present), can better describe the situation, if need be. This shameless act of Flavie's created a hell of problems later with obtaining the child's birth certificate. Not any of *her* problems though!

Also in March 2011, I filed for our taxes. When the tax person (Pacelli Rukundu) had finished, Flavie who does not work but to whom all children monies and the goods and services tax (GST) returns go, said at the last minute that she was filing her taxes separately. She was adamant on doing just that despite all the explications of the tax expert to her concerning the consequences of doing so. And this is supposed to be my life partner that I was sponsoring into Canada? Not only did this reckless comportment cause me to pay again for a new individual tax filing. It also brought about all the hell with Revenue Canada that cannot be sufficiently catalogued here. I am sure that the money for the children has since ceased being paid to her. This is hard earned money that the children are entitled to but her reckless attitude makes it impossible for them to get this benefit of their father's hard work. When this money used to be given to her, it even was always sent to Cameroon: despite that bill payments and other family responsibilities would be burying me alive. Imagine us owing the day-care provider (Garderie Magni Daycare in CDN) but money is being sent to Cameroon because "I am the only one these children [in Cameroon] have".

So (leaving out questions on the children here in Canada), you must be wondering, where then, in her thinking, is my role here as someone who is not only sponsoring these children to Canada but undertaking with the Quebec Government to provide for them for at least ten and twelve years, respectively? Don't be surprised then that this money from Revenue Canada, etc. is the sole reason for her seeking the full custody order she went asking from the Court. Canadian Courts must ask to know what exactly Flavie had in mind when in 2011 she decided against all expert advice to file her taxes separately when we were still living together, and with children. It is all only about getting the money that she does not sweat for and sending to Cameroon. No. The Courts of this country must tell her (and many more people like her) that this is not the proper way to help these children, because my just nicely telling her that makes me a dictator. A dictator whose desire to aid people is so profound that only divine intervention often keeps him from falling further into bottomless pits, trying to help the hopelessly incorrigible.

Classic Divine Intervention: The Liar Mentality and Provoking Comportment

If any of you have never believed in the myriad of divine intervention scenarios in my previous books, then I am inviting you here to make a quick change of heart because you are now entering a Classic Divine Intervention Zone. In Flavie's thinking, the mere fact of having children with me, automatically transforms me into her horse that she can ride anyhow, at any time to anywhere. Capa-Mali, are you there advising her? For example, I have been in this country, province, and city since 1995. All along this period, I had never been to the Regie de Logement. But that hastily changed from 2009 when I started living with Flavie. Despite all her discouraging comportment, I was still determined (as I always am) to help the two children tied to her, brother and sister to the two I have with her (like it or not). But it looks like God Almighty was simply saying 'Peter, I think you're too good to a fault. But I just don't want you to be abused further by some of those you're trying to help'. Those who continue to doubt divine intervention should rethink because that seems to be God's work being manifested through the letter of Citizenship and Immigration Canada (CIC) to me, dated January 24, 2012. 2012! A double liberation year! The liberating letter essentially stated:

Dear PETER ATEH-AFAC FOSSUNGU:

This refers to the Application to sponsor a Member of the Family Class you submitted to this office on behalf of Henriette Flavie Bayiha and family (if applicable). We are unable to process your application as it is incomplete. You are missing the following:

• An original Medical Report Form (IMM1017 Copy 2) signed by a Designated Medical Practitioner (DMP) [of] all the persons you are sponsoring. This must be received at this office by: 03/24/2012.

Your entire application package, along with all requested documents/information, and a copy of this letter must be resubmitted within the timeframes specified above (formatted as "month/day/year"). If you are unable to provide any or all of the requested documents/information, please explain why they are not available.

A pre-addressed envelope label bearing the complete mailing address of this office is enclosed for you to use when resubmitting the application.

When should I contact CIC?

You must notify Citizenship and Immigration Canada (CIC) of <u>any</u> changes to your application. Examples of changes include:

- Changes in your personal circumstances, such as birth or adoption of a child, death of a family member, a marriage or divorce;
- Change of contact information (e-mail, mailing address, telephone number);
- Appointment or change of immigration representative or designated individual;
- Decision to withdraw your application.

You have the option to withdraw your application at any point in the process. You may be eligible for a refund of the sponsorship fee or the permanent resident application fee if processing of your file has not yet begun. ....

Sincerely, Officer PA, Case Processing Centre Mississauga [altered paragraphing for this line]

As you can see, that letter came in, unexpectedly requiring medical reports for her and the two children in Cameroon within a specified period. I say *unexpectedly* because the first sponsorship had gotten to the Embassy and Quebec Government levels without requiring this medical report.

Changes are being often made to the process, of course. Money, money, money, was written all over the unexpected show in town. In view of all the debts and bad credit situations I had already gone into because of her uncooperative and 'what-can-you-do-now' attitude, I simply said to Flavie then: 'You see what I have been telling you all along about sending money to Cameroon when financial problems are choking me here? Now is the real time to urgently send money to Cameroon. Do you have some?'

Flavie always thinks that others are just there waiting for her orders to do this and that for her. I must keep insisting that Canadian institutions now have the unique opportunity to tell her in very strong terms that Canada does not function like that. On the occasion on hand, she did the one thing she is very good at doing. She picked up the phone and called a certain Hugues (a Bameleke relation of hers, she says), told him about the sponsorship jam that she never for a moment imagined could arise, and asked for a loan. Just hear who is asking for a loan: to repay it when and how? Hugues was promptly at 101-5085 Rue Sax, firmly promising to help with the money on a certain date, without asking, in the least, the one who was going to shoulder said loan. I was, of course. I, who was then already down deep in debts and threats of numerous collection agencies, from left and right and up and down. But that is not the only problem. That promised money was going to come when the issue could not be settled within the period given by CIC. Remember that the said children are in Cameroon, not here in Canada. The better option, I thought to myself, was for me to withdraw the file so that the persons sponsored should not be refused because of my failure to meet with the condition and deadline set. Also, I did not want to forfeit the permanent residence processing fee. At that time, I intended to use it to solve immediate pressing financial problems and then file the sponsorships again later. That is, after I must have settled the Regie/rent issue and that of Bell

Canada and others. I clearly communicated this withdrawal decision to Flavie (in the presence of Hugues), and that is exactly what I did, as evidenced by the CIC Letter of February 20, 2012,[12]a letter that was very uncomfortable to the liar mentality

The Liar Mentality

My friend, Me. Edwin Khebila Fogam of Maryland (USA), had suggested and offered to lodge me for about four months, so that I could prepare (with his aid) and write the bar entrance there. I found another 41/2 apartment on Avenue Mountain Sights not far from Rue Sax because I was to go down to the United States as just mentioned. Its cost was $600. 00 per month. As Flavie had rejected the Mountain Sights apartment I put the matter of getting our next apartment into her hands,

---

[12] This February letter stated:
Dear PETER ATEH-AFAC FOSSUNGU:
   This refers to the Application to sponsor a Member of the Family Class you submitted to this office on behalf of Henriette Flavie Bayiha and family (if applicable).
   Your request to withdraw your sponsorship application has been approved. As a result, no further processing of this application will occur. This application cannot be reopened and there is no right to appeal this decision.
   As the Application for Permanent Residence for your relative(s) has not been submitted to the visa office, you are entitled to a refund of all processing fees and any Right of Permanent Residence Fee(s) submitted, minus the $75. 00 sponsorship fee. A refund in the amount of **$775. 00** will be mailed to you at the address above in approximately six to eight weeks.
Requirements for a New Sponsorship
If you wish to sponsor your relative(s) in the future, it will be necessary for you to:
   • Submit a new sponsorship application with all required supporting documentation;
   • Submit new processing fees; and
   • Meet all eligibility requirements for sponsorship. ...
Sincerely, Officer PA, Case Processing Centre Mississauga [altered paragraphing for this line]

with a price range. She then called everyone imaginable, telling them how I have asked her to look for her apartment. Paul Takha Ayah is one of those called and who brought this to my attention. After I had struggled and cleanly terminated the expensive Rue Sax lease ($850. 00/month) by paying off all rent arrears, in April 2012 we moved to a 31/2 apartment ($550. 00/month) on the same Mountain Sights on which Flavie had rejected the 41/2 costing $600. 00.

Just at the time I was about going to the United States (as per plan with Flavie) to prepare for the bar entrance there, Flavie kicked me out of "her" apartment, threatening and stressing that I must leave immediately *with everything of mine.* (Even though I was the one still to be paying the rent, as usual, the lease had been taken out in her name.) Shocked is not the right word to express it. That is how I ended up looking for the 325-7225 Rue De Nancy residence ($500. 00/month). Faced with this situation, therefore, I had to unceremoniously call off the US trip and instead went back to the forest in May 2012. Until this day I have never been able to find the words to explain to Me. Fogam why I never showed up after all the arrangement I had with him, a plan kept alive until the dying minute. All I can say here is that Schola is really a perfect mentor to Flavie. But I am still moving on undaunted, though much slower than I should have; with several persons that needed to be helped, consequently, dying before I had actually found that loving and understanding woman with whom to conquer the world for children.

Two months later (June 2012) Flavie was complaining to me on the phone about this and that with *her* apartment, and that they are not comfortable there, etc. I thought she might have learnt a thing or two. I took time off work and went down to Montreal to move them into *my* De Nancy apartment as arranged. But already in Montreal, Flavie said that she had to wait till month end, whereas she had said on the phone that she was already cleared to leave. I wonder if anyone could ever succeed in doing anything fruitful whatsoever with a person like this. Well, I gave her the keys and went back to Dolbeau-Mistassini. Don't forget that this is the very same drunkard and abusive person, as you have been told. As you can divine, she had obviously kicked me out in April 2012 in order to get into social welfare. But she might then have realized that (not being a sponsored person, as noted in Capa-Haiti's worries above) it was not just as easy as expected. That could now explain why, although ceaselessly complaining about her apartment and how they are missing me staying on their own, she would not move immediately to De Nancy. She certainly was still hoping that the final welfare decision would be positive, but all the same needing to have a backup free-riding plan. A good free-riding schemer, some would say. All these details I never had then, not until she was in Rue De Nancy where her provoking comportment assumed a new dimension.

Heightened Provoking Comportment

The arrangement for Flavie's moving into De Nancy was just that she keeps the phone bill payment up to date so that the service is not cut off again as happened on Rue Sax. (I must precise that whether in Mountain Sights or De Nancy, I always kept sending money to her, as usual; which makes their being in De Nancy more advantageous as she wouldn't have to spend the sent sum or part of it on rents.) I was hardly getting her on the home phone, with explanation always being that they had stepped out. I was therefore calling but her cell phone. I am thus not aware of when she actually moved into De Nancy, knowing only that at the end of the 2012 forest season I return to Montreal in early October and met them there, with everything just thrown around in the apartment as if it was moving day (July 1). I just could not believe how someone could be living with two very young children in an apartment like that. The dangers of being hurt, even to an adult like me, were staring you in the eye. I took to arranging things immediately despite how tired I was from the long drive from Dolbeau-Mistassini.

The phone bill had again accumulated, with threats of disconnection. But that is not all. Flavie began leaving the house in the morning (without telling anyone to where) and coming back late in the night. On arriving, she would disturb especially the sleeping children with her cell phone that rings twenty-four hours of the day. If I ask her to think of the children and inform those always calling her to choose appropriate times to do so, my usual name of 'dictator' is heard over and over. It just got to a point that I told her it was better for her to look for a different place to live in; one where she would assume no responsibility whatsoever, and where no one would ask her to respect simple rules. She asked for time to look for her apartment and I gave her a month. But that period came and went, with Flavie behaving as if nothing mattered, and with the situation worsening by the day. I guess she had been coached and was just looking for the opportunity that her provocation was intended to spark. That is, that I should put my hand on her and get arrested.

They had simply not done their homework (if they do any at all). If Schola of all people never succeeded in getting me to that point, no one can ever do. I had to eventually go to the Regie de Logement and initiate the process for having Flavie leave the apartment because the kids were hardly sleeping, a decision that was rendered on January 29, 2013.[13] It had then

---

[13] The Regie du Logement File No. 31121203057G verdict was handed down by Claudine Novelo, juge administratif, and read :

[1] Le locataire Fossungu Peter demande la résiliation d'une entente de cohabitation conclue avec Bayiha Flavie. ....

[12] **RÉSILIE** l'entente de cohabitation et **ORDONNE** l'expulsion de Bayiha Henriette Flavie du logement.

[13] **CONDAMNE** la défenderesse Bayiha Henriette Flavie à payer au demandeur les frais judiciares de 78$.

dawned on me that Flavie had been in the relationship, using it only as a bridge that had to be completely destroyed as soon as she was on the other side. But why do some of these people just never get it? That is, to live with someone for so long and yet cannot get the smallest clue as to who he/she is? It may surprise others; not me, because I understand this one thing. When you are in a relationship with a hidden agenda, you cannot see what you should have seen, since you see only your scheming as *everything*. Put that as well into the basket of 'The Criminal Love Thesis' (Fossungu, 2014b: 83-85). The question is posed in *Africa's Anthropological Dictionary on Love and Understanding* as to whether you can really love someone and yet not understand him/her. No. It is not love but something else hiding under it – pretentiousness.

Since we were about to *amicably* part ways, the arrangement was that the children would be with me until Flavie can be self-supporting. Also, for the purposes of cleaning up the mess with Revenue Canada that she got us into with her independent tax filing, we needed to mutually agree on which of us was living with the children. Since I was the only one working, and also viewing the disturbance to the children, it was only normal that it be me. (Of course, the money goes straight into our joint account which is practically managed and monopolized by Flavie. Schola would herself vouch that, in her days, I hardly knew when and how much she was collecting for that purpose even as all what she did was pay for day-care.) Flavie even signed a Canada Child Tax Benefit (CCTB) note and other papers on her own volition, which she never sent to Revenue Canada anyways. I made it clear that the process (viewing all the communications from Revenue Canada) would require a lawyer's drafting and formalizing of the agreement,

---

[14] **REJETTE** la demande quant aux autres conclusions.

which she said she would happily sign *"si ça va permettre à ces enfants de continuer à recevoir leur argent"*.

As such, I contacted Me. Jean-Marc Grenier who made it clear that if it was the consensual way I have just explained, then it would cost us a thousand dollars ($1000. 00). But that it would be a whole different ball game if it is to be contested. If I remember well, Flavie was right there as the lawyer and I were talking on the phone, in French. Some days later, when Me. Grenier had prepared the document and requested us to come and sign, Flavie said she was not signing. Me. Grenier then took me for a liar, until I had to show him a copy of the CCTB note Flavie had earlier written and signed. The matter that was supposed to be consensual then went to the court therefore, with two opposing lawyers. By the time we got to the shared custody agreement and I told Me. Grenier to close the file, my bill had gone up to about $2500. 00, if you add all the interests accrued until the bill was completely settled.

Here then is someone with all the family responsibilities and on employment insurance at the time, spending money that he does not even have, and for no good reason. From the discussion I had with Flavie before contacting the advocate, my arranging to even spend a thousand dollars was simply to reinstate the children's money that (it must stressed) was still to go to Flavie. But perpetual liars must obviously be thinking always that everyone else is lying to them, making it extremely hard for the truthful to ever succeed in doing anything with them on board, no matter how much one tries. Anything I tell Flavie as to how we should do things is considered to be my way of deceiving her. Then when she is told the same thing from outside, she is foolish enough to come home and say to me: *"Donc, ce que tu m'avais dit l'année passée c'était vrai. Parceque... [telle personne] m'a dit la même chose hier."* That sufficiently explains why and how we have reached the point we have reached, with the children being the obvious victims. Of course, those who are out there controlling Flavie (in the name of advice) and instructing her not to do what was/is for the best interest of the children, would have also found a lawyer for her. She could then never know just how hard it is to work for the money that she gratuitously spends (or causes to be spent), unless the Courts forcefully bring that message home to her. The people couching and cheering her on, as well as the lawyer they provide her with, just do not know the facts (or, did Me. Gravel have all these documented facts?). And, therefore, they cannot give her any helpful counsel.

Otherwise, they should simply have advised her to get real with her family: like Paul Takha Ayah who seems to understand the situation and has privately counselled her on several occasions, all in vain though. If Paul was not close to me, she would perhaps foolishly listen to him because she would not then think that it is me trying to fool her through him, as per foregoing paragraph. Imagine her "social worker" (for instance) telling her to toss the idiot out and go on social welfare (because in the social worker's head he or she knows Welfare Services would quickly accord her request and then turn around and collect the money from the partner who sponsored her! Join me in saying Shame to Social Welfare Canada!). Flavie foolishly jumps on it. Down the road, nothing is happening as planned: since Social Welfare has now found out she is not in the 'turn-around-and-collect' category. It is only normal, because Flavie herself does not tell them what the reality is. Not surprising at all. If she could not disclose her reality to a person she purportedly wanted to spend the rest of life with, who else would be more privileged to be told that? Put otherwise, was Flavie, for instance, not just in the union to only make children with me so that she could later use them to attain her schemes? Of course, I have personally seen this show before, with Schola, as seen in Fossungu (2014a: 83-99). But I refuse (as always) to judge anyone from another's comportment. That is to say that any woman I might subsequently have to deal with, will have to be the one to let me know who/what she is, not Schola or Flavie. That is my rare perspective on life that has permitted me to learn a lot about human behaviour and other things.

I am not an immigration specialist. But the little I know (quite apart from the advice to foreign students in chapter 3) is that persons who are seeking to get landed in Canada through the refugee door would hardly get that when they get here and only show Canada, from day one to the end, that they are only good at free-riding on hardworking Canadians and permanent residents. I have tried to get this into Flavie's head, to no avail. Even as I began doing the sponsorships, I still advised and encouraged Flavie to still be pursuing her refugee claim, because it is better to have two doors available than just one. Because she was complaining about her 'legal-aid lawyer', I arranged for her to be represented by Me. Michael Dorey, paying upfront the $200. 00 required during their first appointment, the remainder of $700. 00 to be paid after her case was heard. Since that first meeting, the advocate will confirm to you today that he has never again seen or heard from Flavie to date (or, perhaps, he has, only since January 2013?).

If Flavie didn't have it before, I have given her some necessary tools, at least, to be able to get out there and fend for self. I sponsored her *préposé aux bénéficiares* course in 2009 – a field in which I have myself worked. She successfully completed the course. But let us just find out from her if she can show any proof of having ever worked in the field. The list is simply quite long, just as extensive as flaviqueenism that "you should all stand up and welcome ... into *The Hall of (Definitional) Fame*" because "flaviqueenism would clearly merit an enviable place in the *Guinness Book of World Records* and in newer versions of dictionaries" (Fossungu, 2014a: 134). But also come to imagine that I usually take the car along to park it for months in the forest simply because Flavie cannot drive. And all this despite what I said elsewhere that the first gift I

72

ever offered her, a week after meeting her, was the driving books and CD, and requesting her to just show me her driver's licence for me to show her a car of hers(Fossungu, 2014a:130). Why should any able-bodied person like Flavie not be contributing their own quarter, like others, to the Quebec/Canadian economies, etc.? If (like the London one did with Schola) the Quebec Courts and other institutions are interested in assisting Flavie and other women like her in their free-riding enterprises, then, these institutions should not be doing so under the cover that they were not aware of the facts as they actually are – including African immigrants' unrelenting love of the Canadian name-game and other tricks.

Chapter 3

The Culturo-Colour Mixing Theories: African Nosexonomy, The Canadian Name-Game, And The Foreign Students Act On Parliament Hill

It has been discovered that a money-chasing legal profession (as is the case in Cameroon) can hardly help in ameliorating things in this country since it cannot properly defend the rights of citizens and businesses, let alone those of other state institutions, notably the judiciary. That could be the main reason why most of the citizens have simply found it more advantageous to simply join the '*voyous* club' rather than stand up only not to be counted: since no one is there to defend their defending their rights [Fossungu, 2013c: 147].

This chapter and the next deal with the difficult issues of religious, racial and sex discrimination or equality, coupled with cultural mixing that would be creating especial problems of understanding and accommodation between the races, cultures and sexes. Since religion and marriage are rooted in culture, it is important to bear in mind right away that these are inevitably intertwined with cultural clashes, notably that between Islam-derived and Christianity-derived cultures. What about other cultures that are neither of these two? Those too, of course, have been dragged into the show by the 'either-or' posture of the two main contenders. Didn't George W. Bush say it all with his: 'You are either with US or with the Terrorists'? This chapter takes off with the popular name-game and other tricks that foreigners and Canadians/permanent residents use to dodge certain immigration, employment and welfare regulations, also calling for a refashioning of some of the policies to permit foreign students who have studied in Canada to obtain permanent resident status. Niki was certainly not a foreign student. What is as well arresting about her is that all her names are purely African, a fact which immediately brings *nosexonomy* to the mind of an authentic and proud African. But wait a minute! Niki up, Niki down; Niki east, Niki west; Niki beginning, Niki ending; Niki everywhere: why wouldn't I just let go of her as simply as she did of me? Even though I loved her long, tongue-twisting nosexonomist 'first' name, she still advised me to shorten it to Niki, which is what I am obediently doing in this book.

By African *nosexonomy*, I am here referring especially to the fact that most of us sagaciously bear only our African names that hardly officially tell what the bearer's sex is. Some examples are Agbornyor Tanyi, Ngunyi Ateh-Afac Fossungu, Yacubu Mohnkong, Nguajong Forbehndia Fossungu, Fai Ndofor, Tah Techero, and Enongene Ekwe. Does it look like this nosexonomy is one of Africa's neglected "magic portions" to the West? That is, particularly for solving their work-related sex-discrimination: through just knowing a candidate's name on the application. Am I looking forward to finding Europeans being called, for example, Mbinchang Okoro Mandengue? Was Mega Bloks thus using this strategy to discriminate against the men in its hiring process? If African nosexonomy solves the problem of sex-discrimination in Canadian factories, would it also have solved Africa's own infamous ethnic cronyism that is being constantly flashed up now and then as an impediment to unity?

Whatever the response here, I find all the *ethnicity-versus-unity* talk to be the same *we-are-not-ripe-for-democracy* bullshit that is solely meant to opiumize Africans, and particularly the Arab ones (or the Muslim world generally). A lot of ink has evidently been spilt on the issue of religion and democracy in the Arab world; but unfortunately "much of the analysis of the politics of this complex region is cursory or focuses only on today's headlines" (Byman, 2012a: vii). John (2010: 269) has also condemned much of the literature for "being shallow and resting on stereotypes of the [Arab and Moslem people]." The *Islam versus democracy* debate, like the ontological-epistemology debate (see Furlong and Marsh, 2010) that has been elongated into "the quantitative–qualitative 'paradigm wars'" (Stanley, 2012: 97), is obviously one that can hardly be resolved "in a way that all would accept" (Furlong and Marsh, 2010: 209). This difficulty is understandable, especially when one grasps the often unacknowledged fact that both the concepts of religion and of democracy are, in large measures, culturally or socially constructed notions with agendas of their own. And also that most people who advance the religious/cultural arguments exclusively to explain the persistence of authoritarianism in the Arab world often do so while (consciously or unconsciously) assuming a foundationalistic and/or positivistic notion of a 'democracy' reality out there. That is, they present it as if 'democracy' itself is a universally neutral and fixed idea that can be transplanted (as one Cameroonian constitutional critic called HNA Enonchong put it in 1969) from one community to another *in vacuo*, like 'a fungible commodity'. That is exactly where most of the theory would go wrong, in my view.

For now then, I can just give a short answer to the unity excuse based in ethnicity by indicating that in no known country or state of this known world would you find every citizen being of the same ethnic or cultural or religious group. Is Canada itself not an excellent example? Those interested in pursuing this matter further could go and consult Gagnon (2011); Gardinier (2011), Call (2008) and Fossungu (2014b). Africans must therefore say goodbye to those artificial and foreign impositions like Niki's parents did when they *nosexonomically* named her. Could the nosexonomistic theory even begin to solutionize the multitude of factory-associated issues such as the name-game? We would proceed to find that out through studying three topics: (1) nosexonomy's name-thinking in name-thiefing, (2) whether the Halfotwof Logic justifies the American Either-Or Race Theory, and (3) Defending the Foreign Students Act on the Hill.

Nosexonomy's Name-Thiniking In Name-Thiefing While Impossibly Living On New Continents

There is no doubt that nosexonomy has its ups and downs. For instance, if I too had an African nosexonomical first name like Niki, my French-speaking colleagues in MYR (that hub of Africanization in Quebec – Fossungu (2014b: chapter 5)) would not have believed that I was an Anglophone just speaking 'their' French. Most of them have argued tirelessly that I have just learned English in North America (that is, English Canada and the USA), not that I am, first of all, English-speaking. They simply cannot believe that an Anglophone can be as fluent in French as I seem to be (doesn't fearless practice make perfect anymore? Jules-Blaise Komguep, don't I hear you too?[14]). At this point and thanks to no nosexonomy, I would indicate to them that my *prenom* or first name is Peter, not Pierre or something French-sounding. They then are greatly amazed in just the same way as the Americans were when the Arab Spring overturned their self-perpetuating triumphalist delusional 'created reality'. The most important effect of the Arab Spring relates to the shattering of the myth about the Arab's inferiority, immaturity, etc. that belies the Islam-as-inhibiting democracy justification for authoritarianism in the Arab world, a fact that "speaks of the immense human suffering produced by internally and externally initiated, supported, and manipulated violence and instability" (Schnabel, 2003: 1). As Dabashi explains, 'it is that regime of knowledge, that massive topography of emotive imagination, convincing itself that the Arabs and Muslims are constitutionally incapable of even imagining democracy let alone being the principal site

---

[14] See Fossungu, 2014b: 68 n.28.

for inaugurating an event of world historical magnitude, that is now being powerfully challenged (by the Arab Spring), that is troubled by the prospect of losing the ground on which it stands. The destabilization of that regime of knowledge is the first and foremost fact about these uprisings' (Dabashi, 2012: 44).

But there is no need for the amazement from both the US and my Francophone colleagues. Take the US of America first. There needed to have been no surprise. For the United States, Islamism has proven to be a particular conundrum. After the terrorist attacks of September 11, 2001 and the subsequent United States occupation of Iraq,[15] many Muslims – not just extremists – came to believe that the United States was at war against Islam. The election of President Obama, as John Esposito has contended, offered a chance to reset the U. S. position in the Muslim world. Drawing on polling of the region, Esposito found anger at the United States for its policies in the region, even though America's democratic principles are admired there. Indeed, it is the perceived violation of U. S. principles that is behind much of the criticism of the United States (Byman, 2012a: ix). As illustration of said violation, let's take the massive democratic uprising in Bahrain, "the tiny archipelago, home of the US Fifth Fleet, in which that great advocate of democracy, the US, turned a blind eye to the murderous regime in Bahrain, while the UK-trained Saudi military intervened to crack down on the uprising" (Dabashi, 2012: 151). What then is really incompatible with

---

15 Dabashi (2012: 139) sees Iraq as "a glaring example of the catastrophic consequences of trying to 'export democracy. ' If the US had not invaded Iraq and Saddam Hussein was still around, Iraqis might well have been among the first to join the Arab Spring. Instead, they remain under military occupation with their homeland destroyed." Democracy or hegemony, one might ask then? And is it Western-style democracy that brought China to where it is today? And would China be any different from the Western powers, as many Africans seem to be fooling themselves in their sleep into thinking?

what in the Arab world? If the answer is hesitating then one can just know that "Battling Bahrain's Crimes of Humanity" (Matar, 2012) cuts through all the hypocrisy and duplicity that characteristically cloud the true picture of the 'Alliance Structures and Power Blocs' (Byman, 2012b: 68-69) in the Middle East in the wake of the Arab spring.

On the part of my MYR colleagues speaking the French language too I ask: What else do they expect to get from an *Anglo* who could still excel in the UNIYAO in the days when it was the lone Cameroonian university and also completely based on the French educational system, if not its *meilleur* copycat? Dig for more of the *meilleurism* in *Understanding Confusion in Africa* (Fossungu, 2013b), while I continue to begin charity abroad on some new continents to steal a good name for Canadian factories purposes.

Charity Beginning Abroad on the New Continents

Some people just do not give up trying. Some of those disputants of my side of the three-sided coin even had to suggest that I had merely altered Pierre to Peter while in America, in order not to sell myself there as a Francophone (Anglophones in Cameroon are known to gladly do so – see Fossungu, 2014a: 39). Oh, these African Francophones can be so narrow in scope! Shouldn't they have tried to show some creativity by saying instead that I had changed my Muslim-sounding name (that I do not even have: except you want to consider Mbinchang as one) to a Christian name? By that they would at least have given us a little comfort in thinking that they are conversant with some hidden-public parts of American politics that claims religious tolerance. But the way these French-speaking Africans would rather be coming shows clearly that they don't even know that, despite America's melting-pot stance (that seems to be true *only* to its Blacks whose fore-parents were brought there as slaves), French

80

names are still used normally there by people of French decent. Oh, the civic teacher is in real trouble here.

The Civic Teacher's Agony

What exactly have the French taught these African people other than the false greatness of France? Teachers generally are under the ADO (Advanced Democracy Oath) to tell lies to students (see Fossungu, 2013c: chapter 3) but that is not the point here. I am here to talk of the Civics teacher only. I was once given the chance to handle *le cours de civisme* in a Francophone secondary school in Cameroun but in less than two weeks the lessons were withdrawn from me. Reason, you want to know? I was teaching students about their own society called Cameroon/Africa rather than of French emperors, administrative divisions, you name what. Students would be unable to tell you what the capital of a Cameroon province (like Logonezone or Sanagazone or Guinean-Savannazone[16]) is whereas they would – even in their deep sleep– recite to you all the *chef-lieu de tous les départements en France*, including all the past presidents and emperors/kings of that country, and the like of such things. Amazing and unbelievable! Listen to them calling their English-speaking compatriots *les Biafrans*, meaning Nigerians! They don't even know that not every Nigerian comes from that part of the country that wanted to secede in the late 60s to become a new country to be called Biafra. Would you be correct to blame the teachers here when there is "A Truth-Telling Offence in Cameroon" (Fossungu, 2013c: 63-65)? Can you see why Botswana has been praised in an earlier chapter? Don't we say charity begins at home? If you cannot know what is happening around you, how can you *really* know what happens thousands of miles away?

---

16 For more on these new and authentic non-directional names, see Fossungu (2013b: 4; 2013c: 58).

Don't make the mistake here of thinking that it is only a disease of French-speaking in Cameroon. On September 15, 2014 Edwin-Daniel Ndoko posted a write-up on the SOBA-America Forum, which was taking about Deputy Daniel Kemajou having stood up in 1959 against Amadou Ahidjo's bid to acquire *pleins pouvoirs*. You would easily find this history and many others in my writings (especially Fossungu, 2013b; 2013c). The publication of each of these books is always announced in the community fora. From the responses to Ndoko's posting, you could clearly tell that most English-speaking Cameroonians (moreover being out here in North America) were hearing about Deputy Kemajou for the first time. Why is that? It is a sort of negative competition too. They choose to remain ignorant just for the sake, according to them, of making sure someone they know does not become rich with a dime of theirs contributing. I could only then begin to see why many members of the Cameroonian community are always greeting me with the fact that I am a very rich man now that I have written many books. Really? Could someone, please, let them know that money is the last thing on my mind whenever I pick up my power-flowing pen to write anything?

Some of us do what we do for the love of doing it; not so much for the money. If that were not the case, then I am sure I wouldn't be doing anything at all. Why, you are still asking? Because I really do not see that amount of money that could actually pay for what is in this clock-ticking head of mine. Not to say though that money following is out of place. That is a good thing. But the point remains that many of these people decide to remain ignorant just because they think procuring a copy of the books, to know what is therein, makes the writer rich – something they just don't want at all to see happening. Do I need to specify it again to you or do you already see what kind of competition that is? Also do add 'ignorant' to the negative, please, before welcoming them to the new ignorance-jammed planets.

Welcome to Moslema or Islamagood!

Not even knowing basic facts about their own country of birth, how then could they even know how America operates? Anyway, I think I now get it. Eureka! Their *name-thinking* in regard of the USA must be based on the trend they are used to in Canada – adopting (or 'stealing') names for immigration, employment and welfare purposes especially. The issue here is that of name-*thiefing*, if I may be permitted to use some Jamaican here. Jamaicans and other English-speaking Caribbean people perplexed me on first contact, especially in Storex Industries on 9440 Clement in LaSalle. I only grasped what they often said, thanks to my unpretentious and impressive knowledge and mastery of Cameroon Pidgin.[17] Jamaicans and the others say, for instance, that "X come by me house and thief me shoes." No surprise at all to a Pidgin speaker like me. The only astonishment to me was when they would be talking like this to me and feeling really good that they are speaking *English* (or do they call it *Patoa?*). If Jamaicans only surprise me, Quebecers go the extra miles to actually confuse me out of very nice things with Amerench (see Fossungu, 2014b: 34-35), while Zairians hardly pretend with the French language that most of them can barely speak. These Central Africans always prefer to stick it out with their Lingala– one of the possible explanations why they logically love to stick together just as the 'African-but-not-African' Arabs? Answering the query must eventually carry us into the culture-colour mixing theories on our stepping out of the new continents. Welcome to the Religion, Colour and Culture puzzles that are just taking off now.

Most Moroccans and Algerians in Rossy Inc., for example, would tell you that they are not Africans, but Arabs. This makes me to then wonder if someone could quickly want to

---

[17] For a catalogue of the pretence of so-called African 'intellectuals' with this national-unity language, see Fossungu (2013b: 163-166).

find out from them what the hell they are still doing on the continent and also competing in African sports and the like? From this narrative, you can see that they are obviously equating African with the Blackness that they too have come to the continent probably to "whiten" or civilize with their Islam. At this juncture, I then also realize that those Arabs are not alone since it is also equivalent to some (Western) Europeans behaving as if Turks are not Europeans because of their being Muslims. All that then leads me to the theory that whether those denying the plainest of facts like it or not Turks are Europeans until you can and have successfully cut Turkey off the continent called Europe and taken it, perhaps, to the 'yet to be created' continent called *Moslema* or *Islamagood*.[18]

I think this whole thing smacks of the so-called 'clash of civilization' narrative that is undoubtedly 'religion-democracy'-based. Edward Said appears to say it all too clear. Writing about Samuel Huntington's "Civilization Identity" and Bernard Lewis' "The Roots of Muslim Rage", Said (2001) has stated: "In both articles, the personification of enormous entities called 'the West' and 'Islam' is recklessly affirmed, as if hugely complicated matters like identity and culture existed in a cartoonlike world where Popeye and Bluto bash each other mercilessly, with one always more virtuous pugilist getting the upper hand over his adversary. Certainly neither Huntington nor Lewis has much time to spare for the internal dynamics and plurality of every civilization, or for the fact that the major contest in most modern cultures concerns the definition or interpretation of each culture, or for the unattractive possibility that a great deal of demagogy and downright ignorance is

---

[18] As chapter 4 below shows, the feminists will surely call theirs *Feminista*. Yet, they want to have this exclusive world of theirs while still inhabiting *Masculinista*? Similarly, the homosexuals will name theirs *Homonista*; while still paradoxically wanting to also inhabit *Heteronista* at the same time! Yeah America! Your religion and same-sex marriage puzzles are only beginning.

involved in presuming to speak for a whole religion or civilization. No, the West is West, and Islam is Islam. "Yin Song also takes Huntington's postulation to task (Song, 2009: 5-7), advancing many "conclusions [that] openly contradict Huntington's thoughts" (Song, 2009: 7).

Religion has always been, and will continue to be, a very powerful force (for good or for bad) as far as the talk of democracy (governance generally) is concerned. It is actually one of the principal shapers or 'developers' of the democratic ideals: considering the well-known history of the Roman Empire and Christianity that is associated with Western Europe. This is not to leave out the equally familiar competing Islamic Ottoman Empire (tied to Turkey), which Korel Göymen says "provides an excellent example of a state that first undertook reforms in order to reverse an unfavourable balance of power" (cited in Fossungu, 2014a: 26). The 'religious absolutism' of the Roman Catholic Church in confusing or not distinguishing the state and church, reinforced by the notorious inquisitions, the burning of heretics, and excommunications, etc., obviously led to the idea of the requirement of state-church separation, as it is best exemplified especially by the United States (see Campbell and Putnam, 2012; McGarvie, 2000; Black, Koopman and Hawkins, 2011). It is as well responsible for the emergence of norms such as freedom of religious expression that are characteristic of modern day democracies (for America, see Black, Koopman and Hawkins, 2011; and for Canada, see Brooks, 1996: chapter 10). Religion is certainly at the heart of the long-running debate in political science on democratization, as can be evidenced by the fact that 'the West' is now quietly cheering secular Turkey's rise as "The Middle East's New Emperor" (Saunders, 2010) and consequently now seriously reviewing its European Union membership (see, e. g, Daloglu, 2014). The discussion of the Culturo-Colour-Mixing Theories will therefore proceed with the issues of (1) Cameroon's Impossibility Theory versus Arab-

85

Muslim Fanaticism, and (2) whether the *Halfotwof Logic* Justifies the American 'Either-Or' Race Theory(in the second part of the chapter).

Cameroon's Impossibility Theory versus Arab-Muslim Fanaticism?

Like Hasan (2007: 11) has done with the Asian experiences, Byman (2012a: vii) has pointed out that many of the Arab world's problems are not new, and even those that have emerged recently have complex roots in the societies and histories in question; whereas most of the literature is often uninformed by history or theory. The problems tied to the failure to appreciate that 'democracy' must synchronize with the concerned society's unique settings (if it has to be meaningful) is aggravated by the vexed question of how to balance (Western) democracy's generalisation and particularity features. For instance, Owen (2012: xii) sees the problem of "where to draw the line in a world, particularly the Arab world, where everything [including religion] is so closely interconnected with everything else? Also, how [are we] to do justice to [the democracy-seeking] events right across the Arab region where some regimes have fallen, others are engaged in armed resistance to the people's uprising, and others again, as in often-overlooked Oman, have been trying, with some success, to find a way to disarm criticism without any surrender of real power?" That should therefore serve as a convenient *caveat* to those 'quick-jumpers' who want to treat the 'Arab' or 'Moslem' world as a single or homogenous entity with no political and economic and other (time and space) differences. Byman (2012a: vii) also sees changes in the region, and its long-standing complexity, as offering substantial challenges to scholars and policymakers in the years to come because the rise of new actors, changes in the policies and perceptions of long-standing players, and the interplay of domestic and foreign issues have shaken the region and transformed its politics. Could these complexity and interwoven nature of their societies perhaps also explain the Arabs' apparent fanaticism?

The Cameroonian Christian-Muslim Hybrid?

In Canadian factories you will find a lot of Arabs, especially the African ones. Rossy Inc. is one of the places where I met many of them. My Muslim colleagues at work have always behaved as if my not being a complete Muslim (because I am always insisting on *impossibly* being a Christian-Muslim hybrid) makes me an odd nut to crack. The first thing these guys greet you with is always: Are you Muslim or Christian? Like the Americans with race – as seen below – they too think the entire world is just that of Muslims and Christians. I found many non-Arab Africans having a hard time addressing the unnecessary query because, if they were the *first*, they immediately were under surveillance; and, if the *second*, there is further questioning as to why they were not Muslim. Could that be the attitude of all Muslims? I don't quite know and would avoid generalizing. What I do know is that, writing about seven years before the Arab Spring, Schnabel (2003: 2) held that what is required in the Arab world is not the immediate (or even eventual) adoption of full-fledged Western-style liberal democracy, but a gradual process toward more participation in the political and economic life and governance of the various countries, in harmony with religious norms and teachings respected throughout society.

Schnabel's talk of democratic governance in harmony with religious norms and teachings in the Arab world would immediately stir to action those 'stand-still' theorists of Middle East 'exceptionalism' and of 'orientalism' (spearheaded, of course, by Bernard Lewis) who have argued that Arab-Muslim culture is incompatible with democracy (Pratt, 2007: 1). Mark Tessier opines however that both elements, for and against democracy, are to be found within Islam (2002: 340) as in any other religion (Tessier, 2002: 349-350), cautioning therefore that "[a]lthough stereotypes are sometimes advanced, questions about the influence of Islam are appropriate" (Tessier, 2002: 339). The stress though is that "forces of history and economics account for the absence of democratic governance in much of the Arab world" (Tessier, 2002: 340) – a world that the Arab Uprisings have returned "to the mainstream of world history after decades in which they had been largely sidelined by oppressive and inflexible regimes, some ruled by kings, others by presidents who acted like kings in their desire to perpetuate a stifling family rule at all costs" (Owen, 2012: x). While considering Islam's contribution to democracy or lack thereof, I will tend to agree with both Mark Tessier and Roger Owen by taking you back to Rossy Inc.

Gosh! There came the crowd of the North African Arabs then one day posing their familiar Christian-or-Muslim question to me. My answer was: "Both." "Impossible!" they all shouted. You must be either one or the other, they told me. "Then why ask when you know that?" I threw it back to them. It was then that I realized that these North Africans clearly are unaware of "Cameroon [being] the place *par excellence* where the federal structure would not only be dutifully instituted but, above all, also very religiously defended" (Fossungu, 2013b: ix, emphasis is original). These Arabs are simply not familiar with the fact that, for once, President Paul Biya is absolutely right in theorizing that 'Impossibility is not Cameroonian'. As an expert on African politics has elucidated,

Cameroon essentially knows no impossibility in its dictionary of governance. I am here referring to just one of the famous doctrines (*impossibilité n'est pas Camerounaise*) that are persistently churned out of the presidency of Cameroon – the Unity Palace or Etoudi Palace. Some other popular ones are *Un seul mot: Continuer*; and that the truth comes only from the authorities, with anything else (such as this book) being mere rumour: *La vérité vient d'en haut et la rumeur vient d'en bas*. It is with an adequate grasp of this *là-haut* philosophy that readers can be able to comprehend, for instance, what is actually responsible for Cameroon being Cameroon (*Le Cameroun c'est le Cameroun*) and for the impossible not being impossible in Cameroon (Fossungu, 2013b: 1-2, emphasis is original).

I would want therefore to tell these Arab co-workers that Biya is impossibly correct because there is just no *either-or* with Cameroonians regarding these things called religion and ethnicity that often seriously divide people the world over into either-or feuding camps like what one finds in the Middle East. The struggle in this geopolitically important region is mostly dominated by the Shiite-Sunni rivalry. For instance, arguing that Iran could not have played any part in the events that followed the uprising in Bahrain, Hamid Dabashi has made it clear that the British armed forces had trained the very military force that was crushing the democratic uprising in Bahrain, whilst Britain was accusing the Islamic Republic of interference; concluding that this astonishing hypocrisy on the part of the British, however, does not mean that the Islamic Republic is the champion of liberty there (Dabashi, 2012: 150). This is because, to Dabashi, it is clear that the influence of the Islamic Republic in Bahrain is not what the ruling regimes in Bahrain and Saudi Arabia, and their supporters in London and Washington DC, wish us to believe: namely that the ruling clergy in Iran has supported the democratic uprising in Bahrain. Such support, Dabashi thinks, would be very odd indeed because he wants to specifically know why the Islamic Republic would help a democratic uprising in Bahrain while viciously suppressing one of its own. Would it do so just because the protesters in Bahrain are Shi'ite? (Dabashi, 2012: 150). Logically, a critic has then concluded that "[t]he only influence the Islamic Republic had on Bahrain is to teach the ruling regime, by example, how to quell a democratic revolt – the same role it had for the even more bloody crackdown of Basha al-Assad in Syria. There is no ideology, religious or otherwise, at work here, only brute force and self-survival. The same holds for Saudi Arabia and the other Persian Gulf states, for Israel, and for the United States and its European allies. The ideological gloves were now off" (Dabashi, 2012: 151).

All of these things, as I have said, are absent in Cameroon that has more ethnicity than one could even correctly assess (see Fossungu, 2013b: 73-90). No one would need to dispute with the authors who hold that the United States presents a puzzle of religious pluralism, one that "is often personal. And that personal pluralism means that America is graced with religious harmony" (Putnam and Campbell, 2012: 36). Like America, Cameroon is graced with personal religious pluralism as "Ethnic, religious, and cultural tolerance is the order of the day in Cameroon because inter-ethnic, inter-religious, and inter-cultural (*anglophone-francophone*) marriages are very common and regarded as perfectly normal in the country" (Fossungu, 2013b: 200). It should not then be surprising to hear a Cameroonian claiming to be a religious hybrid, as do many Americans (see Putnam and Campbell)? What can the Arabs' 'either-or' questioning really be about? The Rossy Inc. group would further help us after Mark Tessier has discussed Religion and Politics (2002: 339-42) to discover the extent to which religion accounts for variance in attitudes related to democracy in the Arab world (2002: 339). He undertook the study because "So far as democracy is concerned, some observers, particularly some western observers, assert that democracy and Islam are incompatible. Whereas democracy requires openness, competition, *pluralism, and tolerance of diversity*, Islam, they argue, encourages intellectual conformity and an uncritical acceptance of authority" (Tessier, 2002: 340, my emphasis). The Arabs' attitude towards the Black Africans in Rossy Inc. could ally these theories but I truly also wonder what pluralism, non-conformity, tolerance, etc., do actually mean to this advocated-for democracy when, as Al-Muhajiroun would specifically claim, "the Jew and Christian will never be happy with you

90

until you follow their way of life" (cited in Wiltorowicz and Kalterthaler, 2012: 131).

Nicola Pratt's book also challenges deterministic and essentializing approaches to theorizing democratic transitions in the Arab world by examining the dynamics of authoritarianism and of opposition to it as a historically constituted political process (Pratt, 2007: 2). Tessier (2002: 340-41) further indicates that many other writers have rejected the suggestion that Islam is an enemy in the struggle for accountable government, stressing that both elements, for and against democracy, are found within Islam (Koran), as is also common with the Christian Bible, I would add before calling on Rossy Inc. again to attempt some possible explanations. You already know that I met some Guineans and other sub-Saharan African co-workers in a night club called Balatou where beer was all over the tables. So, how could one explain the Guineans (at the same workplace with me) saying at work that, as Muslims, they do not drink beer? Does their being Muslim depend largely (if not exclusively) on the presence of the Arabs whose religion these Black Africans are practising? These are questions that had also been lingering on my mind especially in connection with the 'Alhadjis' of Cameroon, who are always carrying a kettle around with what they say is their tea. Is it really tea in there or alcohol? The Guineans thus set my mind working hard: No beer-drinking under watch but otherwise out of view! Religious Hypocracy or what? Should I not be entitled to conveniently question this further under 'the halfotwof logic', as seen below? This Black-Muslim hypocracy is even accentuated with the pork-eating thing.

The Rome-Adage Thesis, the *Viande Hachée* Theory and the Hot Dog Argument

The hypocracy in this whole beer-drinking matter leads me to wonder if this is an issue also of cultural assimilation/adaptation in dissimilar cultural environment.

That is, the popular saying ordaining that 'while in Rome, do as Romans'? This is quite tricky. As Fossungu (2014b: 179-195) wants to know: Does that saying mean that while in Rome an African, for instance, has to *unAfricanize* and *Romanize*? If so, why do Europeans not *Africanize* while in Africa? It all seems to be a power thing, with the strongest winning always. Let's hear, for instance, what Funnyman has to say about *viande hachée* (ground meat) in the MYR camp when I wondered aloud why Africans with very strong and active teeth should always be given meat without bones, and moreover ground beef, all the time. He expressed much surprise that I (that he regarded as the sage of the camp) did not know why. Saying there are many reasons, Funnyman decided he would give just two, leaving me to help myself thereafter. I was grateful and made that known. "First", Funnyman indicated, "Mario is not foolish. He is preparing to soften our teeth that might eventually bite him. In that event, he would not feel too much pain. " He paused for a while, hoping the message sinks in. Whenever this guy speaks, especially when relating to anything I have specifically brought up, he always makes sure to go 'nice and slow' like Elton John sings in one of his tunes. I just don't know if the guy had divined long before that I was going to put his thoughts into anything like this book, as I am now doing.

Second, Funnyman resumed after seeing how I was nodding my realization, "you should have also asked why we are always given rotten or near rotten fruits (apples, oranges, bananas): if you didn't know Mario to be an excellent exploiter of Africans' *mouton* comportment." What did he mean to say *au juste*? I asked in the manner of the journalist. Unlike my cousin, Desmond, Funnyman certainly understood the dynamics and did not first get upset when he coolly responded to my 'audience-in-mind' query: "That *viande hachée* is just another form of the cheap unhealthy and dangerous meals we are served with and taxed for by MYR." I was really posing questions in my mind as to whether or not this funny guy could compare with Charly in that science called Blackology. "By the way," Funnyman interrupted my roaming thoughts and concluded, "that ground stuff could contain just anything beef-like, including the pork (or even *cochon*) and the numerous vehicle-hit animals on Chemin Bowater that some of us claim not to eat!" Funnyman ended there and there was much laughter as always. His mention of *cochon* quickly reminded me of a drunklampostist argument.

The Hot Dog Argument with Paplé: One early morning a guy got to the MYR kitchen-restaurant and asked for four *saucisses de cochon* in his menu. It was the first time I was hearing that since it is always *saucisse de porc* that everyone (except the Muslims) asked for. It was quite funny then. There is this Burundian that is considered to be a *paplé* (insane) from the consumption of marijuana or "le médicament", thanks to a Zairian supplier in the camp. Paplé made it clear that morning that they in Burundi do not eat *cochon,* eating only *porc.* I found an issue with Paplé's thesis, loudly indicating that both were the same thing. Paplé and I argued heatedly for a while. But, through some third-party's intervention, I realized that *cochon* in French would be referring actually to the one in the bush with protruding teeth; what Cameroonians call *bush-swine.* I had learnt something from Paplé that I could never have grasped from the way Francophone Cameroonians wantonly use *cochon* abusively. Any little thing, *Cochon*! Whoever said 'the theory of drunklampostism' was a useless theory? At that point I was seriously thinking of Charly's 'careful listening' advice in regard of drunkards (Fossungu, 2014b: 225-27) when my initial impression about French-speaking Canadians and their *Amerench* surged forward. But I decided to pose my own question after Funnyman's enlightenment. So, my little final thinking-aloud query was: *Na wu fit tell me sey me weh I say I no di chop nyamagoraw neva chopam?* In other words, who can then prove that I who claim not to be a snail-eater have not actually eaten snails? Welcome to Senneterre!

Senneterre Welcomes A Guinean Villager

Once more, Welcome to Senneterre! Our Senneterre trip in September 2014 was memorable in very distinctive ways, including the provision of a non-*ben-ben* or straightforward response to the last quiz. We were staying in town while making the two hundred or so kilometres into the forest to work, having our meals at Resto Centre-Ville which is on 630, 10e Avenue. No more camp in the forest also meant no more *amata*, no more 'mountain of food' although quality taking the place of quantity. That quantity-quality stuff was irrelevant to the *amata* lovers though; and this is where most (if not all) of the Burundians/Rwandans fell really sick. No more milk (*amata*) was an unthinkable occurrence and, as Funnyman laughingly theorized, "consider that Resto-Centre-Ville ashes if that ever happened in the MYR camp!" I have also heard Salihou Dabre wondering on several occasions whether children are born in those two countries with an *amata*-feeding bottle in their mouths. These Burundians/Rwandans in MYR do in fact drink milk just like water: morning, afternoon, evening, night, and perhaps even in their sleep! As Salihou then concluded in Senneterre, they just drink that much milk because MYR makes it available *en vrac*. Otherwise, he questioned, "how many of them have you now seen buying milk? Do you think they drink it like that in their homes? If you say yes, then I must assume that they must be in a constant and vigorous competition with their kids every day!" This Burkinabe guy does not usually talk a lot. But when he speaks he makes a lot of sense.

Of course, the white *contremaîtres* and other workers were always segregated on their own table(s) as they do also in the camp kitchen/restaurant. I therefore don't know their stance; but *débroussailleurs* were generally dismayed in Senneterre, feeding-wise *surtout*. They were however afraid or shy to speak out. But just hear Peter Ateh-Afac Fossungu requesting the lady to increase the quantity of rice in his plate, indicating clearly and firmly that he is not an idler in town but "someone who has just returned from cutting hectares of the forest." Lynn Leclair (the manager and owner) immediately asked how much we were being paid per hectare and Fossungu nonchalantly responded: "I don't know." She immediately fired back that the hungry man ought to know and then got the *shock* of her life when Fossungu coolly said: "Yes, of course, *I* ought to know. But *you* don't have to know that!" Her negative view of us (African *débroussailleurs*) that must have been occasioned by Diallo the first day apparently altered and the food quantity thereafter augmented noticeably. She also changed and became as nice as any sensible business person should be to their clients.

On our very first arrival at this restaurant where we were to be eating during our time in Senneterre, this notorious Muslim guy from Guinea (Diallo, *le grand coupeur*) proudly and contemptuously walked up to the restaurant management and declared: "*Moi, je ne mange jamais le porc! Je dis Jamais!*" It was so shameful to many of us the way this guy still comported himself in town as if he were still deep down into his forest world of MYR that is practically out of Canada and in his very small and backward village in Guinea. Two or three days later this guy also came into the *resto* and was going straight to be served food when the manager told him he had to first sign the *facture* and his rude response was: "*Je viens d'arriver!*" I could not help jumping in to publicly find out from Diallo if the fact of just arriving entitles anyone to eat without paying? He was just as mute now as he had been on that first day after another trunk-cutter, in the person of the restaurant owner had inquired from him: "*Le simili-poulet que tu manges chaque jour là, penses-tu que c'est quoi au juste?*" The lady had gone on to explain that it is just half chicken in there, the rest being *pork*, etc. That is why it is called *simili-poulet*[19] Diallo is said to have later on declared to his West African Muslim entourage that "I don't give a shit if I have already eaten pork!" Ah, this pork thing everywhere in the MYR camp! Oh, this American either-or race thing!

The Halfotwof Logic Justifying The American 'Either-Or' Race Theory?

In my researching for the race/colour mixing theory I have learnt a lot on race from Yin Song (2009: 10-11) who prefers "the term 'hybridity' or 'hybridization,' because the three equivalent terms [like *métisation*, creolisation, and mestizaje] have limited connotations and the word 'hybridity' encompasses most diverse intercultural mixtures, including racial, linguistic, historical and geographic realms. " He takes the time therefore to explain the other terms, letting us know that creolization "originally stands for the mixture of African and European culture in Caribbean and North America. In Hispanic language, creolization refers to those of European descent born in Americas as against the peninsulares born in the Iberian [P]eninsula and [N]ative Americans. "[20] Also citing the works of Whiten, Jr, N. E. and A. Torres titled "Blackness in the Americas", Song (2009: 10) indicates that "Mestizaje is a wider Latin American word in relation to boundary crossing mixture. The term served as a hegemonic elite ideology and the doctrine of racial purity. Latin American nations are supposed to achieve modernity by the "whitening" or Europeanization of their population and cultures. " This whitening talk brings us to the colourless colour.

---

[19] See also Stéphane Dassault, "Une charcuterie faisait son bœuf haché avec 3% de porc" *Journal de Montréal* (26 septembre 2014), 7. For the trick, the company was slammed with a fine of $750. 00.

[20]Song (2009: 10), citing Pieterse's "Globalization as Hybridization".

The Colourless Colour and the Halfotwof Logic

All the trouble has been taken by Yin Song to show us therefore why Americans are always talking as if the world is just that of black and white. And then Michael Jackson in one of his moving tracks is singing that it doesn't matter whether you are black or white. Nice try, M. J., but really? That is O. J. Simpson asking, not me. I remember the day the O. J. decision was handed down in 1995. I was at McGill. This McGill expibasketism again! I was really amused by the reaction of the large LL. M. class that had just three Blacks (a Kenyan gentleman called Hannigton Ukomu, a Nigerian lady in the person of Annastasia Gbem, and myself from Cameroon). The white students were all in complete shock that O. J. was found 'not guilty' as charged. Asked about what I thought of the verdict, I made it clear that I was rather surprised at their surprise because it clearly told me that, to them, there is justice only when a Blackman like me is unjustly condemned, not when he is justly discharged. One of them, a very pompous American, asked what I meant and I stated: "It seems to me that because O. J. has been found 'not guilty' you no longer have trust or faith in your justice system that is considered the world over as the most robust. Or, am I wrong?" He merely walked away without another word. Hypocritical white people, you would say? Don't jump-start the group stereotyping thing or anything like it. But what is this colourless colour thing all about?

The Ku Klux Klan-Dubious Logic (KKK-DL)

I am wondering here because we hear so much talk about "the rights of people of color" (Crehan, 2013: 67) and "an elderly man in a wheel-chair with someone who appears to be his son and a woman of color with her two small children" (Crehan, 2013: 67). Colour down, without colour up! What is going on? Are there even white people? This question may seem extraordinary but I have to ask it because the only time many of us see white people is when they are in their Ku Klux Klan attire. But then it is the outfit that is white, not the one putting it on. Have you ever thought of that? Do most homosexuals not emulate this KKK-DL? That is, homosexual in hiding and heterosexual in public? Blacks seem to approximate their assigned colour, especially if you look at their hair. That is what I have been taught from childhood to call black. But, again, hair alone is not the person. What would s/he be called when the hair changes to grey? From black man to grey man, you would say? What about 'white' people with black hair? And how about classifying those of them with blond hair too? And what is to be said about fair-complexioned 'blacks' like Mariah Carey? It is here also that the American tendency of classifying anyone with even one percent Black blood as Black really puzzles a lot of people. A Métis (French for Latino Mestizaje?) and a Black can never be the 'same': unless you want to tell people that the offspring from a pig and goat is a pig. I am not a good biologist but let us just call Métis what they are: Métis. Not Black, not White, as the Halfotwof Logic attempts to show.

The Halfotwof Logic

A Métis is half-half of two races. Hybridization, as some would say. "Hybridity is generally interpreted as syncretisation, creolisation, and mestizaje. In the early 1990s, Arjun Appadurai used the term—creolization—to expound the interplay of cultural hybridization" (Song, 2009: 10). We can here also use the Halfotwof Logic to expound the interplay of genetic-colour hybridization. Some critics have posed questions to know why the Black part usually dominates in the Métis. Is it because of the better approximation thesis just noted above? Is it most probably that? I find the questions quite compelling because in secondary school I learnt from my colours tutor that combining black and white brings forth charcoal grey and that black and yellow leads to something close to black. Was my tutor wrong? And what is responsible for the fact that two Blacks are able to bring forth what is called an albino, like Yellow Man? What is the difference between an Albino and a 'White'? I do not know all of that but I know that different things cannot be the same, except we want to give a different meaning to same like the homosexuals – gays and lesbians, as they love to be referred to. My suggestion is that nature already differentiated them. Our further differentiation is consequently artificial. Let us just deal with the differences as they are without further differentiation or *undifferentiating* and the world would be a much better place for the different peoples inhabiting it, including the clean-and-clear polygamists.

The Marriage MPPEP Equation: Monogamy Plus Polygamy Equals Polygamy

Despite Song's (2009: 12-15) questioning of Tomlinson's cultural imperialism theory, I am sure that what is involved with the religious marriage practice of most Africans can scarcely be cultural hybridity or métisage. I am talking about the marriage theorem which is behind the funny Métis or Halfotwof Logic. We are to use it, of course, to demonstrate that the condemned artificiality-creation does not leave out the African world of hypocritical mixing, as seen in the Marriage MPPEP Equation. The Black Muslim's attitude in regard of beer-drinking already noted would be no huge surprise to you if you also think of the Catholic Africans in the presence of the priest and other church officials, especially in the marriage sphere.

DOMA Definition of Marriage Equals Heterosexual Monogamy

For the purposes of Neil Westbrook's study "marriage", like in the DOMA (Defence of Marriage Act), "refers to a traditional or historical view of marriage as a legal or religiously

99

binding, lifelong, monogamous relationship between one man and one woman" (Westbrook, 2010: 8). Debra L. Delaet and Rachel Paine Caufield find it to be inconsistent that most religious conservatives opposed to gay marriage in America embrace religious liberty as a core value but they paradoxically urge for marriage to be defined as "a union between one man and one woman." They cite President George W. Bush, in a 2004 speech, calling for a constitutional amendment that would essentially make the DOMA part of the Constitution, strongly articulating his view of the need to defend the traditional meaning of marriage:

The union of a man and a woman is the most enduring human institution, honoring—honored and encouraged in all cultures and by every religious faith. Ages of experience have taught humanity that the commitment of a husband and wife to love and to serve one another promotes the welfare of children and the stability of society. Marriage cannot be severed from its cultural, religious, and natural roots without weakening the good influence of society. Government, by recognizing and protecting marriage, serves the interests of all (cited in DeLaet and Caufield, 2008: 306).

Today there are more than 1500 different faith groups in the United States, a multiplicity that prompted Greeley's labelling of America as "the denominational society" (Smidt, 2011: 106). But President Bush obviously does not know all the so-called cultures and faith groups he claims to be speaking for. For instance, to leave out faraway places for a while, what has the president to say about marriage between 'one man and more than one woman' as practised by the Utah state's Mormonism? Wasn't that what was once demonstrated in *Reynolds v. United States*? Is it therefore not simply a question of 'religion deceiving through comforting' (Westley, 1992: 346)? That is, trying to religiously impose one's limited worldview on everyone? That is a completely till-the-end-of-the-world issue that Edward Said and others have already plunged themselves into.

The important issue about the definition right now is that my father, for instance, was a staunch Catholic. The Catholic Church is one of the most outspoken religious denominations not only against SSM (same-sex marriage)[21] but also polygamy. But just look at the number of wives he ended up with, simultaneously most of the time! Again, no big surprise to me, since I realize that he is a royal. The astonishing thing though relates to why these Africans cannot tell whoever is bringing their religion to them to either make it palatable with their (Africans') customs/cultures or disappear with it? In discussing the historical background of the social institution, Westbrook (2010: 10) has stated that "Any consideration of marriage or Christian marriage in particular must take into account the fact that marriage historically defined as a sustained, recognizable relationship between a man and one or more women predates recorded history and is rooted in the very origins and life of humanity itself." Polygamy then is not a recent invention.

Adopting or Faulting the KKK-DL?

If (mark you, I say if) polygamy is inherently part and parcel of African tradition, why must Africans embrace a religion (which is part and parcel of some other culture) that proves incompatible with polygamy? This thesis seems to be at the heart of the tussle between the Arabs' (and the American)

---

[21]Like many other Christian denominations, the Evangelical Lutheran Church in America (ELCA) and the Baptist Church have been communities polarized by the question of same-sex marriage (Jungling, 2007: I; Westbrook, 2010). It should be noted that 'polarized' is used, not 'dead', because even religion's staunchest critics are "impressed by the toughness and resilience of religion, in the face of what they considered to be overwhelming odds" (Westley, 1992: 329; also Baker, 2012). Laurie Jungling and Neil P. Westbrook are obviously right about the polarization within several faith groups that has been occasioned by same-sex marriage.

Either and *Or*, thus excluding any room for peaceful cohabitation. It is amazing that (Black) Africans embrace a religion that preaches against 'many wives' (or beer-drinking) in preference of 'one wife' or alcohol abstention. Yet they want to have both, one openly and the other in hiding? Is this the KKK-DL strategy again? Just see what they end up becoming: neither Europeans/Arabs nor Africans/Blacks. They are rootless and dangling uselessly! We have just heard George W. Bush making it very clear that *Marriage cannot be severed from its cultural, religious, and natural roots without weakening the good influence of society.* What then is that culture in which this hide-and-seek marriage is rooted?

Or should I say the Africans in question become a 'Cultural Métis' – the Halfotwof? That too could not be the case. "Cultural hybridization is an ongoing process in which the effect of economy and politics on culture increases the complexity of cultural hybridization studies" (Song, 2009: v). But for John Tomlinson, Song (2009: 12) admits, "the idea of cultural hybridization is one of the most deceptively simple-seeming notions which turned out, on examination, to have lots of tricky connotations and theoretical implications." Therefore, by borrowing from Foucault's notion of discourse as power, Tomlinson established his own concept of cultural imperialism and adopted it to evaluate the effects of cultural interaction; viewing cultural imperialism as "the use of political and economic power to exalt and spread the values and habits of a foreign culture at the expense of a native culture."[22] Bringing it back down to our Marriage Equation, the *Marriage Métis* too could be out of the question (quite apart from the P's dominating the equation): because 'one wife' *plus* 'many wives'

---

[22] Song (2009: 12), citing John Tomlinson, *Cultural Imperialism: A Critical Introduction* (Baltimore: The Johns Hopkins University Press, 1991), 3.

is 'many more wives', never a hybrid between the two.[23] Does that equation then also justify the American *either-or* thesis on Métis? If you think so, are you not then clearly saying that the Métis is not a Halfotwof since s/he has more black genes (the dominant: 'the more than one wives') than white ones (the swallowed-up: 'the just one wife')? If that is indeed your theory, then it might also be validating the albino origin thesis and, therefore, the white's too? Short, that Adam and Eve were Blacks?

White imperial priests particularly are not going to like this, for sure; and neither would the Muslims like them for *democratically* looking down on their own equally imperialistic religion. This leads to the inevitable clashes between competing imperialists for the soul of the 'religionless' African(?), with much exposition of double standards on both sides as could be seen in the Christian religion's sacrament of marriage in chapter 4. Until then, my advice is that Africans and other 'uncivilized' peoples of the world had better be 'civilization-savvy' with these wolves in goat skins in the same way as some of them have proven to be Canada-savvy with the name-game. You see this easily in the Muslim-infested factory called Rossy Inc. where I even became odder to the Muslims when I often posed questions to know why the authentic Muslims that they say they are should be disrespecting the 'Muslim Sunday' by

---

[23] The seemingly successful localization of Starbucks and the newly emergent anti-Starbucks campaign in China revealed China's current struggles in cultural identity in the process of cultural hybridization. Neither total socialist or total capitalist, modern or postmodern, China's hybrid culture embodies the fundamental tensions and contradictions of globalization (Song, 2009: 1). But the arrival of American fast food in Chinese market did not diminish the popularity of authentic Chinese food. The co-existence of traditional Chinese food and American fast food has proved to be complementary. Moreover, the globalization of American fast food suggests that a new mixed social, cultural and economic form has been configured. What is interesting in this case is that American fast food restaurants took in German hamburgers, French fries and Italian pizza, then reproduced and promoted in American style (*id.* 9)

coming to work on Friday. There is often no straightforward response given here; they just wallow left and right and disappear, leaving me with more time to gently lead you to the conclusion of the name-game.

Didn't someone like Meiway (the West African singer) or Fossungu (2014b: 49-55) tell you that Cameroon's Bameleke would do anything under the Sun to make money? I knew a Bameleke guy in the same Rossy Inc. who had a very Muslim-sounding name (both first and family) and who would be a sure Gold-Medal winner in beer-drinking and pork-soya-eating in an Obili bar in Yaoundé. This Cameroonian could only compete with just two others in the factory, one Zairian (whose work week was 'officially' Wednesday-Friday) and the other Latino who sipped his stuff even at work, looking drunk all the time. Of course, you know by now that I am not saying that all Muslim people actually avoid alcoholic drinks and pork. I guess the principal point is just that if in school in Canada you know me as 'Moise Kikijimedou' and then meet me in a factory where everyone is calling me 'Pédro de Lacruzilez,' you had better just be Canada-savvy not to start asking: 'I thought your name was. . . ?' That is the popular game foreigners (especially students) and welfare recipients play in Canada because of its somewhat twisted immigration policy that would necessitate my defending the enactment of a clean-and-clear Foreign Students Act.

Defending the Foreign Students Act On The Hill

I will first tell you what the Foreign Students Act (FSA) consists of; then advise prospective foreign students before going into details supporting the enactment of the Act. The FSA requires (1) the granting of permanent residence to foreign students who have completed their programme in a Canadian institution and duly applied for it; and (2) the according of an open renewable work permit to them after the first year of studies (for those whose programmes last more than a year). I know some people would be saying that these things are already available. To that I say *lie-lie*. What is in place is just not good enough, or what they think it is. Let's leave ben-ben or circuitous things behind and go for straight-talk or fossungupalogy with our precious foreign students through (1) *grandes ambitions* and silly thieves and (2) saying adieu to *roundaboutism*.

Advising Prospective Foreign Students: Competing *Grandes Ambitions* and *Silly* Thieves

Should the FSA not be put in place, then here is my open non-roundabout counsel to prospective foreign students aiming at studies in Canada. My Dear Foreign Students: Instead use a minute part of the enormous amount you are to pay as differential fees to get yourselves "lines" that would bring you to the shores of Canada as asylum claimants. Even if at the end you are not accepted (most unlikely), you would still have *chopped adoro*. To *chop adoro*, as Ghanaians would go on to better explicate to you, means that you claim asylum (based on real or fake dangers in Africa, for example), get into social welfare or *aide sociale* and then, most probably, join the *travailleurs au noire* club forever. Sucking Canada Dry from both ends, that is. To properly understand how it works, also hear President Mobutu out there in Europe addressing Zairians in Lingala and advising them to steal as much from the white man as he has been doing from these poor Africans. In short, Mobutu is asking them to 'chop adoro' by lying that he (Mobutu) wants their heads. Both speaker and listeners think they are well covered. As foolish as Mobutu, you would say? Lingala is a language that any savvy person can learn within a couple of weeks. I did not need to do that to know because Zairians themselves gave me the information in Rossy Inc.

Why shouldn't stealing become a national trait in Zaire when Number One Zairian does that bidding? Didn't embezzlement also become a national government style in Cameroon when Paul Biya asked a journalist who was pointing accusing fingers at a minister: "*Est-ce que vous avez des preuves?*" Of course, we need proof for every accusation. But is it not for the courts to demand for that evidence? What does the Cameroon president actually mean then? That he is judge and player, for sure. That could also explain why he alone can decide when to put any of his stealing/embezzling "collaborators" behind bars any time and any how without any court or person asking for proof: since he always has a 'stealing dossier' on all these so-called collaborators.[24] '*Grandes Ambitions*' thieves obviously know one another, you are saying? What a combination that would then result from *Grandes Ambitions* and *Silly* thieves! Do not get me wrong. This is not to say that every Zairian is idiotic, with all Cameroonians having questionable great ambition. When Thomas Eyoum'a Ntoh describes Cameroonians as 20 million rascals (see Fossungu,

---

[24] Talking of having a dossier on collaborators certainly warrants your enjoyment of an expibasketic invisible dossier. As a supervisor in Rossy Inc., the manager and other supervisors (a Moroccan and Zairian) knew well in their heads that I too had a *dossier* on them. On many occasions I had stumbled on the gang stealing company goods and loading into their cars. It was not any of my business since the company certainly did not hire me as a security guard. But they were nervous and their numerous ploys to get me into the group were in vain. But when the Ontario Court sessions attendance brought the long-sought opportunity for them to get rid of me there, the 'invisible dossier' largely played into the very favourable terms of the 2006 'Agreement Between Peter Ateh-Afac Fossungu and Dollarama LP' "to determined precisely the terms and conditions related to the termination of employment of Mr. Fossungo for the company. " The implicated manager happily signed the agreement as 'Employer', with Marc-André Fillon from the Head Office signing as 'Witness'. I, of course, signed as 'Worker'. Without the *invisible dossier*, of course, I would simply have been slapped with some sort of high-handed and one-sided termination letter, like the Lockwood Manufacturing warning letters of 2003 (see Fossungu, 2014b: 46-48). The unseen dossier thus put me in a better position to bargain with my killers who happily did the killing softly.

2013c: 146 n.153), it is not like every Cameroonian (including this writer) is a *voyou*. But that alone does not fault his thesis. Only 20 million rascals would actually allow one head to think for them for over fifty plus years. No surprise then that "At a glance one would say that almost everybody in this 'Green-Girl' country [called Cameroon] is an infant [in politics]."[25]

That said, is this debate after all not even raging between going from one African to many of them or from many to one Africa? Unlike Congolese who also speak Lingala, Zairians are said to be lazy and with long hands. I have never lived in Europe but that is the echo from those who have, including my Rossy Inc. Zairian informants. I need not rely solely on those European echoes because I have some first-hand corroboration. I was living in a building in LaSalle (Boulevard Bishop Power) where a lot of them were occupying a 4 1/2 apartment opposite mine. But for the simple fact that they were Blacks who were always speaking Lingala, I would have quickly mistaken these Zairians for Chinese. I used to marvel at the exact number of persons (of both sexes) living in the apartment *en face de mon appartement*. It is usually none of my business to pry into people's lives. But when every time you open your door you see several different adults getting into an apartment facing yours, there is every reason to be concerned about who is, or is not, your neighbour. This is the more so when we have to remain the socialists that we Africans are.

African Socialism: Teaching Americans to Care?

It was my daughter's baptism and I had invitees, also having invited every tenant of the building to the occasion. That is what Africans generally do. In addition to eschewing the normal jealousy of money-crazy white neighbours, Africans generally share in both grief and joyous events. I do greatly

---

25 Peter Ateh-Afac Fossungu, "Who Is an Infant in Cameroon?" *The Herald* (Cameroon) (10-11 February 1999), 4.

107

appreciate a lot of our African values that we maintain even in our homes away from home; very unlike the so-called "advanced" people. Achal and Tangonyire (2012) have explained the money-crazy phenomenon well, in positing that selfishness becomes more prevalent as a people move from elementary economic systems to modern economic systems; arrangements that are plagued by what Fletcher (2011a) castigates as "The Famous (and Almost Never Understood) Theory of Comparative Advantage" that is solely meant to conceal "De-moralizing Economics" (Ferguson, 2006: 69-88) and 'What Economists Will Not Tell You' (Rodrik, 2010: 61-66).

Some of these critics think that the major reason why economic systems collapse is human selfishness. Otherwise, they find it hard to understand why, despite all the achievements in science and technology, there are still money-poor people in the world, with environmental cataclysms having become daily occurrences. They attribute the problem to the would-be agents of development, such as multinational corporations – MNCs (who ever deceived you here?[26]) – and states that are largely motivated by selfishness (you're now talking). Unfortunately, they continue to narrate, poor economies pursue development using borrowed models formulated for selfish reasons. (Is Africa carefully listening here?) Needless to say, the solution to current economic and environmental challenges does not lie in abstract Keynesian economic jargon or more advanced technological machinery but in taming the evil of human selfishness. These experts' vaccine against the virus of selfishness, they say, is education for altruistic egoism (Achal and Tangonyire, 2012; Mentan, 2012; Eagleton, 2011).

---

[26] "[T]he complaint against global institutions," James (2009: 3) writes, "is that they are too strong or too interventionist, that they detract from national sovereignty," with this being very pervasive in Africa especially.

Yes, Mentan (2012) could be correct in concluding/suggesting/predicting that socialism is the only practical alternative to contemporary capitalism. Teach them then what Africa has to offer in the field because it is all about money to these white people; leading to Thomas Edsall's important question: "Does Rising Inequality Make Us Hardhearted?" In answering his own query, Edsall (2013) states that "[o]ver the course of American history, support for economic redistribution has been the exception, not the rule." Just imagine how all this happens because of their *ben-ben* or crooked view of socialism. Of course, it is no secret that I should be the one to divulge, that Americans have been brainwashed by the Military-Industrial-Complex and its offspring Complexes into thinking of socialism to be "a rough proxy for interventionist government", which explains why it is viewed "negatively by 60-31" Americans (Edsall, 2013). No doubt a lot of people do condemn these white people for seeming to think, drink, breathe, eat, reflect on, nothing else than money, to the extent that anything not money-geared is counted as zero. The white man's disease then seems to have become the adorable norm, according to the Blackologist. That would begin to explain to you, according to the others, why these people are always so stressed up, with no one to even come by to say hello. And they then get so surprised (and jealous, you may add) seeing their African neighbours having so many members of their community not only visiting all the time but partying and supporting each other also in stressful situations.[27] That is African Socialism that cannot be deterred

---

[27] You get a better sense of what I might here not be saying clearly from late Vivian Beng's *thankyouology* to CGAMers on November 22, 2006: "Dear goodwillers: I wish to thank you for the overwhelming support you gave me while I was hospitalised. The visits; the telephone calls and especially the family card that was sent to me in my sick bed actually took me away from that bed back home. Special Thanks to the president of goodwill. I do appreciate and owe you brothers and sisters of the goodwill family. Thanks again. Yours Vibeng"

or effaced even by *moneylessness* and the boundless distance away from '*The Dark Continent*'. Let There Therefore Be Light On The Darkness!

What said white neighbours often then do (to avenge the fact that these '*moneyly* backward' Africans have what their so much money cannot even buy for them) is to call the police to stop the parties or other gatherings (and there is hardly any *AITWsian* gathering that is not a party of some sort). Not that the gathering is actually disruptive of the peace in the neighbourhood, but the police often would not bother about that for obvious reasons that President Nelson Mandela would have helped in telling you if he were still here with us. But you know anyway. A female Guinean friend at one of such occurrences wondered to me if money alone, without people, could one day be able to take care of even burying such stressed-up money-chasing people. I did not quite know how to respond to her but told her I was working on it, looking for experts on the issue. I then found some friends of that science with not only "The Theory That's Killing America's Economy" (Fletcher, 2011b) but also with "Dubious Assumptions" (Fletcher, 2011a) that is noted for fooling people into thinking that money stores values. What values are not values, the African is here asking?[28] I will therefore let Achal and Tangonyire (and the others) to try explaining things further to

---

[28] This book hotly disagrees with Ferguson's (2008: 358) painting of financial markets as "the mirror of mankind, revealing every hour of every working day the way we value ourselves and the resources of the world around us." It agrees instead with the German president who argued not long ago that financial markets are 'monsters that must be put back in their place' (cited in Ferguson, 2008: 358). The values of Planet Finance surely do not reflect those of anyone else but of those few who belong to that greedy planet. Although capitalism has been of a global character since the 1400s, the current phase of globalization is manifested by emergent transnational institutions, changing relations between multinational corporations and assaulted paradise of sovereign nation-states and the development of a global monoculture of consumption among feuding class divisions (Mentan, 2013a).

my perplexed party friend while I focus on talking to you about my Zairian neighbours.

Like many of the invitees, the Zairian next-door multitude was there. There was much to eat and drink. They were all seated together and rather than having fun there like all others, hear what they were doing instead, to comprehend that a perpetual thief will steal even what is already given to him or her. Women and men alike, they would each make endless trips to their apartment with bottles of beer in their clothing. I behaved as if I did not know what was happening. That is what Crisebacologists do to be Crisebacologists (see Fossungu, 2014a: 24-29). To me, they were not stealing anything except a lot of the returnable bottles that made the no-return voyage. These Zairians! I now see why they love working where we were with their late dictator's son. Don't be puzzled to learn that I have even personally met a Mobutu son in one factory here in Montreal that assembles computer and other electronic parts. I would have doubted his being a Mobutu but for the fact that he was a real carbon copy of the late dictator. This is the kind of company that you would find Zairians completely dominating in. How did they feel being there with Mobutu's child? As they elucidated, they love him because he does not see eye-to-eye with his father, and the like of such bla-bla. These Zairians think everyone is as childish as they seem to be.

The National Thiefing Strategy

When these Zairians find a factory like the one we were in, they make sure every Zairian who is around and willing gets there. It is not so much about Zairian solidarity or Zairian love. It is solely about not having a non-thief in the midst of thieves (Rossy Inc. supervisors, are you there?). The presence of this kind of person is dangerous to the *Thiefing* Brotherhood. Imagine being there and keenly watching these Zairians in order to understand them. They then take that for your being someone who can easily denounce them. Since all the heads or supervisors in this scenario are Zairians, they then make sure the agency (Kelly Services) does not send you there anymore. Preventive strike as George W. Bush would say in regard of Iraq? Israel too does it all the time against the Arabs and no one dares call it terrorist attacks? The Brotherhood justification is regularly heard.[29] Of course, behind the Iran/Brotherhood cards is what Baker (2012: 216-222) describes as 'The Islamist Imaginary', explaining that "Imaginary of course refers to something conjured up in the mind's eye, in this case, the powerful, threatening Islam of the American imperial project" (Baker, 2012: 216). If other authors are not clear enough on the point that the US of America *et al* would see Islam as a formidable stumbling block to their hegemonic and homogenizing agenda, then Raymond W. Baker is when he posits that

Islam has established itself as the only transnational force able to resist America's homogenizing power on a global scale. It has inspired the most successful Arab resistance to the American-backed expansion of the Israeli state. Extraordinary popular revolutions in the spring of 2011 in Arab lands, though not led by Islamists, evinced a distinctive Islamic collaboration. The ordinary Muslims who made these revolutions, notably in Egypt and Tunisia, framed their mobilizing calls for freedom and justice in an Islamic idiom rarely appreciated or even

---

[29] In discussing 'False Anxieties', here is how Dabashi reacts to the issue of Israelis fearing the Muslim Brotherhood's rise to power in Egypt: "Of course both the Israeli prime minister and his like-minded Iranian ally [Albas Milani] habitually ignore the fact that more than sixty years ago a 'Jewish Brotherhood' had created a Jewish republic in the same neighbourhood. Soon after what was in effect a joint statement by Netanyahu and Milani, Ali Khamenei, the leader of the Islamic Republic, celebrated events in Egypt as a reflection of the late Ayatollah Khomeni's legacy and duly hailed the commencement of an 'Islamic awakening. ' Not so fast, interjected the Egyptian Muslim Brotherhood almost instantaneously: this is not an Islamic revolution, but an Egyptian revolution that belongs to all Egyptians – Muslims, Christians, and other of different ideological persuasions" (Dabashi, 2012: 147).

112

understood in Western commentary. As people took to the streets by the hundreds of thousands, calls celebrating the greatness of God mingled with those demanding the end of tyranny. This improbable assertiveness of Islam in so many unexpected ways is the central and little-understood paradox of the Islam in our time. How at a time of such unprecedented weakness has Islam made itself such a powerful transnational force? How has an Islamic world in decline and under attack succeeded in initiating a centrist, global wave for renewal? By what alchemy does Islam translate the visible weakness of Muslims into a formidable wave of Islamic resistance? [Baker. 2012: 197-98]

This thesis from Baker ties in perfectly with President Bush's elaboration of a strategy of global hegemony in 2002 in a document called 'National Security Strategy of the United States', by which the United States would never again allow a hostile power to approach parity with U. S. capacities, and it would take the offensive to ensure its continued dominance (Baker. 2012:216). American Secretary of State, C. Rice, was obviously propagating this policy when she declared in 2006 in the Middle East that the region's borders will be redrawn since, to her, existing ones did not mirror the people's wishes and aspirations. *Wuna just year me sum theen*! Is Ms. Rice here talking of the Arab/Muslim's aspirations or America's hegemonic interest?

Whatever it is, I wonder about what the *Zairian National Thiefing Strategy* was in that factory. That is, what exactly the heads/supervisors would commonly have told the agency dispatcher about you. That you are a thief, obviously? I wonder even more about you being a foreign student who has just *borrowed* or *thiefed* the name with which to be in there "trying your best" and have been screwed up by these adoro choppers. Now, my Dear Foreign Students: Just imagine the vast amount of money that Canada would have spent on you (as an adoro chopper) before sending you away, compared to what you would have squandered in Canada as a foreign student and at the end be told to go back home before attempting to immigrate to Canada! You will be the winner in this scenario, except that you would not have studied. But having been accepted as a convention refugee (most likely), on the other hand, you can thereafter study for practically free as a Canadian Landed Immigrant. What happens to those who want to play 'fair game' with Canada?

Accord Them Permanent Residence and Open Work Permit and Say Adieu to Roundaboutism

To be on the savoir-faire side of things therefore, Canada should strive to make it a win-win affair for both foreign students and Canada. It makes absolutely no sense that foreign students who have spent so much in Canada are hypocritically excluded from permanent residence by this country's roundabout policies, while those who have instead paid out money studying elsewhere are favoured. As an expert on the issue has explained it,

For instance, job opportunities in my field (university lecturer or other positions in the public service generally and the professional guilds) are directed only to Canadian citizens and permanent residents; and to become a permanent resident, I would need to show that I have that job. That is for people like me who have already spent so much studying and living in Canada. But someone that has instead studied, say, in Belgium and wants to become a Canadian permanent resident is very advantageously welcomed, not being saddled with this roundabout exclusion that I had squarely tasted before graduating from McGill University in February 1997 (Fossungu, 2013a: 144 n. 15).

This Canadian policy really reminds me ('*Je me souviens*') a lot about the Cameroon Goodwill Association of Montreal (CGAM) membership politics, with the playing around *outstationism* (out-of-station membership) particularly exemplifying. No membership category of that Association has received more controversy and misapprehension than that of out-of-town. Existing members who relocate out of Montreal could retain CGAM membership as out-of-town-members, with the following conditions applying: must attend at least one monthly meeting session in a year (paying a fine of $50, in case of default); must contribute towards all financial obligations, including death; exempted only from monthly contributions towards entertainment and parties if not present. The controversy arising from this membership category is two-fold: Participatory Lukewormity and Diehardity, and Convertible Roundaboutism.

Participatory Lukewormity and Diehardity

Lukewormity and diehardity are intimately tied to the End-of-Year (EOY) party. The issue of ticket sales is a very important one here and tells you much not only about lukewormity but also about the membership dynamics that Fossungu has been pushing against to no avail (see Fossungu, 2014b: chapters 5 & 3). This is in connection with the leaving of membership open to just anyone who feels like walking in and out at their own pleasure. I will shorten the discussion by just letting you listen to the 2013 CGAM President, Caren Osong Ayah, talking about lukewormity/diehardity and '*The Future of Goodwill*' on December 29, 2011 when (as then 2012 Vice-President-Elect) she discussed some of the party issues:

Hello Chair [Fidelis Folefac]: I use this opportunity to congratulate you for a job well done during the EOY party. The party was a success and we all had fun, that we can't deny. Through this email, I want to raise some points that I think we should closely examine. These points are explained below.

1) The fact that about 1/4 of Goodwill is made up of out-of-town members I think is something that we should reconsider. Most of these out of town members we never see

them present at one of our meetings with the exception of Mr. Denis Alem and Mme Ayuk Etah Cecy. I think if out-of-town members want to maintain their status, let them be able to attend at least one or two of our meetings during the course of the year without which they lose their Goodwill membership. Let us not continue to dwell on the fact that we have members when for 2-3 years we have never seen them in our meeting sessions.

2) I think it is a shame that more than half of the Goodwill population would deliberately not sell tickets for what we all call 'our party'. If members don't sell tickets, how do we expect to make any profit? It's not enough that Goodwill would sell only 247 tickets for what we all call a grand EOY party. Look at it from the point that each member would have made an effort to sell at least 2-3 tickets; it would have made a big difference. Those who labour themselves to sell tickets are not stupid neither are they jobless.

3) During our parties, Goodwill women are ashamed to serve food to people and to this effect we always see 'self-service' by the guests. In other parties like BASA MPOU, BINAM etc., their women stand to serve food to their guests. So why is the case of Goodwill different? If we don't change this habit, then in one of our parties let's be prepared to experience severe food shortage.

4) I think in Goodwill we have two kinds of members, namely, 1) die-hard members and 2) luke-warm members. The die-hard members are those who work tirelessly for most of the parties that Goodwill has been organizing while the lukewarm members sit and fold their arms for every party. This is not acceptable and we have to change this behavior. Let us know that the success of Goodwill is the collective effort of its members. There are many ways that we all can contribute towards a party. We can either commit in selling tickets or commit to help with the organization of the party or commit to ensuring that the party is going smoothly in the hall e. g.

116

picking up plates and bottles or commit in ensuring that Goodwill properties are removed from the hall after the party. Let us note that these die-hard members who have been organizing most of the parties for which we all take credit would experience burn-out. To this effect, I am moving a motion that either Goodwill should stop organizing parties or we have new members aboard who will then take over the organization of parties.

On January 1, 2012 Fidelis Folefac made it known to 'Mme V. P.' that "[t]his is straight talk which should constitute a framework for the continuous improvement of Goodwill. I am glad that it is coming from someone who is a member of the 2012 board. I am hopeful that the 2012 team will seek ways to address these and related concerns. " I think it is such things that, looking back, would make 2006 the year of achievements for the CGAM, as the 2006 president (Paul Takha Ayah) rightly put it in the year's well known January Assembly where he presented the ground-breaking *'President's Vision for the Year 2006'*. As Fossungu (2014b) has shown in several of the CGAM General Assembly discussions, it could thus not be the out-of-town members that are really the problem; it is the *in-town* members and their *adhocist* changes we should be pointing fingers at. Let us take for instance the 'membership-status-crisis' created by the Hans Najeme government of 2007. The president was being congratulated later from left and right for having resolved the problem but I think most of us were negligent of the role of the dedication of the concerned out-of-town members that was the most important factor to the resolution issue. Peter Ateh-Afac Fossungu did not fail to bring this out in his own reaction to it on July 16, 2007 when he had stated:

Mr. President, Dr. & Mrs. Tambong,

It's very unfortunate that we got into the messy situation in the first place; but it feels really good to know that the air has been very cordially cleared. I still fondly remember my words to Dr. Tambong when I saw the very distinguished couple at our last Mothers' Day Party: "How I wish Goodwill could love you guys just one-tenth the way you love it!" Dr. Tambong just laughed and threw back this "Pineapple" at me: 'Are you going to throw away Ngunyi, your child, simply because she, in her child-like ways, insulted you?' The answer was obvious and uncalled for so our discussion quickly switched to other topics. I have always known (but on that day this knowledge was concretely cemented) that, for this couple, it was – to borrow Mr. Anung's apt words – 'Goodwill forever'. But still I must join my voice in the chorus to say congratulations to our President for a job well done and to the Tambongs for always comprehending.

Yes, it was largely due to the wonderful understanding of the outstationists. But Willie Nelson, if I remember well, sings that there must be an end to understanding. So, it is not the out-of-town members that are to be blamed as I said earlier. Were it otherwise, how do you then conveniently explain convertible roundaboutism?

Convertible Roundaboutism

On October 4, 2009 Rita Ebude Ewane (then Secretary-General) rightly followed the *Law of Outstationism* when she wrote: "Hi everyone: As we are all aware, I am no longer in Montreal for professional reasons. I would have liked to continue to serve Goodwill as ever before, but, helas! Nonetheless, I would like to be recognised as an out-station member henceforth. Paper work[] will follow. " The January 2008 General Assembly records also show that Fai Ndofor appropriately requested a change to outstationism when he relocated to Quebec City, just like Cecilia Ayuketah before him. As indicated, the former Secretary-General and these other members (including, as of October 2006, Sarah Takang (to Calgary) and Georges Neba (to Germany)) clearly were on track.

This has not been the case with two former CGAM officials. On May 11, 2013 Edward Takang Ayuk (CGAM 5th president) wrote asking to switch regular membership to the out-of-town status whereas, interestingly, he clearly was not out-of-town. Here is how he himself put it: "Hi All, Good day and accept hearty greetings. I am currently out of town and will be travelling most of the year. I would be more than grateful to assume the Out of Station Membership status effective Thursday May 09, 2013. Thanks for the usual co-operation and understanding. Warmest Regards [altered paragraphing]. " No one from the Executive Bureau said anything as to the inappropriateness of this request for conversion, which leads me to the conclusion that the conversion request was blindly granted, as usual. For instance, Emilia Efode Tambong of Gatineau wrote on August 3, 2009 "to suspend my membership in the Association effective today August 3rd 2009, until further notice." Secretary-General Rita Ewane was quick to request on August 4 for her "to kindly follow the right procedure."

Similar to the former president, on October 29, 2011 Pius Esambe Etube (former financial secretary) indicated that "I travelled out of Montreal to Calgary two months back (August 30th 2011). It's not a permanent relocation but it may turn out to be so. Consequently, I would like my status to be changed to an Out-of-Station Member. I am not sure if Notice by way of email is the correct procedure. Where this is not the case and I [am] required to complete a form, then I would like to have the form. Best regards. Pius Etube [altered paragraphing]. "There is no indication in the records that this request too was rejected (or corrected as President Fidelis Folefac lengthily did to Wilson Anung's suspension of membership in 2008[30]) as

---

30 On June 28, 2008 the president extensively addressed the S-G's *resignaspension* to 'Dear goodwillers,' first indicating that "[f]ollowing an

should have been the case. You simply cannot be out-of-town when you are not out-of-town. The appropriate option for this *two-exampled* scenario was to suspend membership. The two former officials did not do the right thing most probably because they had their eyes on the social packages or *sociopackism* (for elaborate discussion of which, see Fossungu, 2014b), yet wanting to avoid monthly contribution! That is real convertible roundaboutism.

While roundaboutism is here being used in the CGAM to avoid responsibilities that go with membership, the same concept serves the Canadian government to exclude foreign students studying here (call them the Participatory Diehards or Toft's "Refugees as '*Diamonds*'") in preference of people who chose to study in some other countries than Canada and/or come here only to suck Canada Dry (that is, the Participatory Luke-worms or Toft's 'Refugees as "*Locust*"). My counsel is that a foreign student who has completed his/her studies here should be able, if that is his/her desire, to apply to be landed in

---

executive consultation, below is a statement of clarification of some of the issues raised in the letter of resignation and suspension of membership." Dear All, it began:

> We do respect Mr. Wilson Anung's decision to resign from his position as SG of Goodwill and to suspend his Goodwill membership. It is his inalienable right to do so. However, in his resignation and membership suspension letter made public via the group mailing list, he did evoke certain issues that should be adequately cleared for the interest of the association. It is in this regard that we provide you these explanations.

> **Duration of membership suspension**

> We will like to recall that Section 6.7 A (i) and (v) of Goodwill Constitution call for a **duration** of suspension of membership and possible extension thereof respectively. So it is not possible to indefinitely suspend membership in Goodwill. Also, to ensure proper transition he will be audited in application of article 12 (c) of the constitution.

this country without the further hassle of having to return to their country of birth to do so; nor having to show proof of a job already obtained when obtaining that job is tied to permanent residence/citizenship! This is even more than convertible roundaboutism; it is *hypocratic* exclusion; disguised apartheid, to be specific. Otherwise, do landed immigrants from Europe, for example, have to show proof of having secured a job in Canada? If so, then why were the *trio* arriving from Belgium that this writer personally took to Lockwood Manufacturing in 2003 (see Fossungu, 2014b: 46) without a job at the time they got to Canada?

The advantages of facilitating the landing of foreign students that have successfully finished their programmes in this country are numerous. For example, rather than Canada spending on them as it does to asylum seekers, they instead spend in Canada, with the universities of this country also being the winners. With the institution of these clean-and-clear proposals, these academic institutions would also become veritable competitors for foreign student enrolment – the principal source of revenue for them. There is more and more and more; but especially there will be a drastic reduction (if not complete eradication) of the abusive power of the capagivists that you have seen in chapter 2. This also prevents the predicament of children that are brought into this world solely as intimidation and money-getting devices. If in this way this book helps in cutting down the number of such children in Canada particularly, it would have attained one of its main objectives. The operation of the current regulations is not smart, the more especially with the issue of permanent residence. I recognize that the work permit case has been ameliorating over the years; going from work limited to campus in this writer's foreign student days to select summer employers, etc. The really big news came with the June 1, 2014 changes that now grant full-time registered foreign students the right to work 20-hours/week maximum. Bravo Canada!

But much more is still required. Make it an open renewable work permit, in my view. This type of work permit should be granted to them particularly after the first year of study. There is no doubt that some critics would argue that when they get this work permit they would abandon their studies. I say NO. First, renewability obliges showing proof of still being in the programme. Second, coupling it with the permanent resident status suggested above meditates against that; instead being a motivational factor for programme completion. Third, that permanent resident status and the permit also better aid them to avoid the negative competition that is couched in the lack of "Canadian Experience" (see next chapter). Having a work permit given to foreign students as suggested here not only solves the 'experience' problem. There is more to it because no matter the quantity of money they bring along to study, after the first year a foreign student must be dry in Canada. It is not for nothing that there is this drink called Canada Dry. That is why it is being proposed that these students be allowed to legally work anywhere in Canada, especially after their first year of studies and be given permanent residence on completion of studies, if they choose to apply for it. That takes a lot of illicit power of some ben-ben people off their neck, also aiding them to avoid engaging themselves in the illicit name-game and paper-enticing enslavement from scholizyvettist capagivists who are known to use the sex or mbombo trap a lot.

Chapter 4

Sex Politics And Foolerrandism Or The Eko-Roosevelt Dance: Different But Treated As Same And Same Seen Differently?

No one subject appears more consistently in the work of early European sociologists than that of religion. Durkheim, Marx, and Weber each wrote extensively and movingly on the question of religion, and their works seem to be driven by the same basic questions. What is the source of the awesome power that religion can have over the mind of believers? What are the consequences of religion for social life? What is the origin of the inevitable tension that seems to exist between the religious and secular spheres, the sacred and the profane? What is the future of religion? [Westley, 1992: 329]

Another apt replacement to the second part of this chapter's title could be 'From Feminism to Homosexuality or From Feminista to Homonista in Masculinsita-Heteronista?' The chapter shows that feminism began denying the natural differences between the sexes, and thus gave the homosexuals some ammunition to carry the denial to its extreme conclusion. That is, both groups want to eat their cake and have it at the same time; the feminists wanting to have their exclusive world that one may venture to call *Feminista* while still living in *Masculinista*; and the homosexuals theirs of *Homonista* while still inhabiting *Heteronista*. All these instances cannot fail to create or invent puzzling puzzles for the traditional institutions of marriage and of religion. Sex and colour (race) have no strong rivals in the domain of discrimination. Their strengths and weaknesses in the field can be conveniently compared to those of religion's hide-and-seek marriage to democracy especially in the Middle East.

An important challenge made clear in *Religion, Democracy, and Politics in the Middle East* is the likelihood and risks of weak governments in the Middle East, which are magnified by the Arab Spring. Non-Arab governments, like Turkey, Iran, and Israel, remain strong, with Israel and Turkey also enjoying tremendous military and economic power as well as political stability. Byman (2012a: x) sees the possibility of the other regional governments remaining militarily second-tier; with some, particularly those without oil to bolster their bottom lines, also to face significant economic difficulties that the Arab Spring compounds. As Daniel Byman further makes clear, weakness is likely to be the dominant characteristic of Arab governments in the years to come. He sees some, like Egypt and Tunisia, as essentially establishing new political systems and institutions after years of political decay under the old regimes. Countries like Jordan and Algeria that have not seen regime change are either trying to co-opt the forces unleashed or defy them. In all of these cases, Daniel Byman thinks that their primary focus will be on shoring up their position at home, with foreign policy probably reflecting domestic concerns rather than strategic ambition (2012a: x-xi). Civil wars also represent the most extreme form of weakness. For example, Libya entered a civil war shortly after the Arab Spring commenced, with NATO intervention tipping the scales in favour of the opposition and leading to Qaddafi's downfall. Meanwhile in Syria and Yemen, and perhaps elsewhere in the years to come, Daniel Byman predicted regimes slipping toward extreme unrest and civil wars mostly because of the transnational identification common in the Arab world, which would easily make the case for such civil wars easily spreading or drawing in outside intervening powers (Byman, 2012a: xi).

Landing back from the Middle East Democracy Expedition onto the sex that African men seem to love so much, can Mega Bloks, for instance, justify its hiring more women than men on the basis that most of the tasks there are what women are better at doing? Are there tasks there that are uniquely women's own? A further discussion of situations similar to these questions could be found in Brooks (1996: 326). To begin with some responses to the probing, I think I understand women, as Elton John (of all people) would say. I have obviously lovundeleared them a lot at various stages of my complex life to be able to lay some claim to comprehension (see Fossungu, 2014a). "You really think you really do?" That is Colin Diyen, the wife consultant, questioning me because it is his belief that "such men [as me who] claim to fully understand what is on a woman's mind at every moment, [exhibit] an indication of control over the female sex, and proof of their opinion that a woman's happiness depends fully on the man. Do men really understand and know as much about women as they presume?"31

The wife Consultant is absolutely correct and I deeply regret not having consulted with him before now. I can now admit that I don't think I have been able to comprehend especially women working in Canadian factories. You saw earlier in chapter 1 that in Dynacast Inc. none of them ever was pot-man like Collins and me. Most of these women in the 'out-of-home' factory would ask a man to carry heavy stuff for them because "I am a woman and it is too heavy." But why do they rush to cry foul when the man is to be paid more for having more muscles? Is that not a clear case of *Eating Your Cake and Having It*? What do the feminists and others have to say in response? The postulations of the feminists could be best described in Cameroonian musician Eko Roosevelt's popular dance called *Go For Before For Back*. I will therefore try delicately journeying with you on/along the famous Feminista-Sex 'eat-your-cake-and-have-it' Highway with (1) Feminism and Foolerrandism and (2) whether Americans should emulate Canada in the domain of Gay and Lesbian Rights.

31http://www. langaa-rpcig. net/Wife-Consultant. html

Feminism And Foolerrandism

Randall (2010: 114-135) and Brooks (1996: 325-356) have lengthily discussed feminism, which is difficult to define, let alone to provide an agreed definition for (Randall, 2010: 115). This is most probably because it originated outside academia as an ideology of a critical and disruptive social movement. This largely explains why its absorption into social, let alone political, science has been partial and selective and there remains a gulf between feminism 'out there' and feminist political science (Randall, 2010: 114). Political science, being a male-dominated age-old discipline (Randall, 2010: 124-134; Brooks, 1996: 327-330), it has, unlike most of the social sciences, remained "remarkably undaunted by the feminist perspective" (Randall, 2010: 134) largely because of feminism being "too radical, too exclusionary, and too judgmental" (Ferguson (2010: 247). Randall (2010: 115) discusses some of its many versions or perspectives like Liberal, Marxist, and Radical, including the barrage of critical responses to feminist political science (Randall, 2010: 152-154). Ferguson (2010) sees the criticisms just noted above as giving birth to "choice feminism", a version which clearly brings to the foreground the confused nature of the feminist approach; a fact that seems to give "mainstream political science" lots of credit for not "paying much attention to it" (Randall, 2010: 114) as an approach or theory in the discipline. This discussion will thus proceed with (1) Foolerranding Choice Feminism and (2) Asking Gays and Lesbians if like poles no longer repel.

Foolerranding Choice Feminism

While recognizing the impact of feminism on political science (see Randall, 2010: 117-152; Brooks, 1996: 356), many critics are inclined to regard feminism more as 'perspectives' than an approach or method in political science. As Michaele Ferguson puts its folly out there for all to see,

choice feminism offers a worldview that does not challenge the status quo, that promises to include all women regardless of their choices, and that abstains from judgment altogether. Moreover, it enables feminists to sidestep the difficulties of making the personal political: making judgments and demanding change of friends, family, and lovers. Yet judgment, exclusion, and calls for change are unavoidable parts of politics. If feminists are not to withdraw from political life altogether, we have to acknowledge the difficulty of engaging in politics. Political claims are partial; we will inevitably exclude, offend, or alienate some of those whom we should wish to have as allies. The political concerns and dilemmas to which choice feminism responds are very real. However, we can take seriously the political motivations behind choice feminism without withdrawing from politics. Instead, we need to complement an acknowledgment of the political dilemmas facing feminists with a celebration of the pleasures of engaging in politics with those who differ from and disagree with us (Ferguson, 2010: 247).

This passage reminds me much of many things, including *foolerrandism* and Quebec's separation politics, not leaving out the CGAM's April-Fool democracy (see Fossungu, 2014b: chapter 4). I am not tackling all those here but I know you are evidently wondering about what foolerrandism is. Well, you can conveniently substitute it with *Eating Your Cake and Having It*. Writers such as Dani Rodrik talk of globalization's conundrum in the sense that markets have demanding prerequisites – and global markets even more so. As Rodrik further explains it, markets are not self-creating, self-regulating, self-stabilizing or self-legitimizing. States are therefore indispensable to the operation of national markets but they are also the main obstacle to the establishment of global markets because their practices are the very source of the transaction costs that globalization has to surmount. That, to Rodrik, is the central conundrum of globalization: can't do without states, can't do with them! This thus renders the quest for a perfect globalization a fool's errand (Rodrik, 2010: 21-23).

What I think Rodrik and others failed to visualize is that the globalization conundrum holds true only to trade within and between democratic and/or sovereign states. Only a sovereign state (in the legal and behavioural senses – see Nahar (2008) for distinction and definitions) can be able to affect those transaction costs discussed by Rodrik (2010: 10-21). African countries not being in that sovereign category or club, here is what we get the specialists telling us. The multinational corporations' "Dreams of Avarice" (Ferguson, 2008: 17-64) would then "have become the unflinching articles of faith" (Akokpari, 2001: 189) that are designed for making "Uncertainty of Values" (James, 2009: 231-77) in the South in order that Nobody must be "Watching 'Big Brother'" who mercilessly tramples on "the Protection of Cultural Rights in Present Day Africa" (Oloka-Onyango, 2005) at the same time as 'Planet Finance' is creating "Human Bondage" (Ferguson, 2008: 65-118) in its unhindered 'Assault on Paradise' (Mentan, 2013a; Oliver, 2001). China could prove all these interconnected theses, thus adding its own fair share to the globalization paradox – the sure reason for the big boys now hating their very own rules? What about making the personal political too from the feminists that would also appear to be a case of hating rules?

Making the Personal Political or Making 'Opposite Poles' Not to Attract?

The passage from Ferguson on foolerranding choice feminism also reminds me of the lengthy discussion of 'The Personal Is Political' (Brooks, 1996: 244-346) which signifies "that the fight for gender equality had to be waged in the workplace, the media, the schools, and over women's bodies [which] struck a responsive chord with many" (Brooks, 1996: 345). But do we not think that the feminists do take it too far by refusing to acknowledge the plain fact that "men and women were very unequal in life" (Brooks, 1996: 325)? Feminism began denying the natural differences between the sexes, thus giving the homosexuals some ammunition to carry the denial to its extreme conclusion. Indeed, they seem to overdo it because, as most of the critics would agree, "Men and women are biologically different [and a]lthough obvious, the social implications of this simple fact have been the subject of enormous controversy" (Brooks, 1996: 327). Yes, Stephen Brooks, you are exactly right. These feminists seem to surely want a world of theirs called *Feminista*; living in this exclusive world of theirs while still inhabiting *Masculinista*? Do they not complicate our understanding here just like the double-talking in the Middle East by outside actors also does?

Some critics see the duplicity as complicating our understanding of this critical region and making development of effective policy more difficult. Both understanding the region's history and anticipating how the revolutions shaking the region will change politics are vital, according to Byman. In the end, however, he thinks outside actors will shape regime policies in the years to come far more than will foreign intervention (Byman, 2012a: xi). It is quite true that outside actors will do a lot of the shaping to achieve their own goals at the expense of those of the Arab Spring. In 'The East is West, the West is East' (Dabashi, 2012: 144-46) Hamid Dabashi argues essentially that 'the West' has been so contingent on 'the Rest' that when the 'the Rest' decouple from it to discover their own renewed pact with history, 'the West' will not know what to do with itself. So the glory of Syntagma and Tahrir come together to rename 'democracy' on an Athens-Cairo axis. On that basis, the very idea of 'the West' will disappear from the face of the earth (p. 146). That is probably what 'the West' fears and would be prepared to do just about anything possible to prevent the decoupling? Otherwise, how can we explain off the 'admirable' Interaction of Democracy and Islam in Turkey (Göymen, 2007) in the context of the Islam versus democracy narrative? Is it not clear that it is only western capitalist interest that is involved here? What do the feminists and others have to say too in response to their two-worlds living?

Sexism and the Home Factory

Just tell the feminists that they can't simultaneously live in both worlds and they will tell you that it is sexism, thus creating a situation where "a lot of the male participants were finding it awkward to even say what was on their minds" (Fossungu, 2013a: 61). As Brooks (1996: 344) explains it, sexism was coined in the 1960s as a label for behaviour that treated males and females unequally for no good reason than their sexuality. Sexism in its numerous forms and wherever it took place, he concludes, was the target of the women's movements that emerged during these years. To further demonstrate, let's just take that other factory called home now. I am looking at my babe (*umogorey*, according to Burundians) lying on the sofa and am feeling the great urge because of her beautiful and tantalizing Niki-like breastwork that (poor me!) I don't have anywhere on me, and because of which I am *Collinsianly* dying for her. Oh! How all-knowing God must be to think of difference! Yet, my wonderful Rwandan *umogorey* regularly throws it into my face (every time I am trying to exercise my right as her 'opposite pole') to strictly watch out because "we are the same!" Good Gracious! That is my late dad saying it. In Quebec we rather quickly say *Tabernacle*! If that is not really a lot of my late mother's *millingho* or things that would make you laugh to breaking point, then why am I going after her? Don't like poles repel anymore? The soul-searching query here seems to be more intensely directed to the homosexuals.

Gays and Lesbians: Like Poles No Longer Repel?

Is the sameness in my *umogorey's* thesis because *man* is in both woman and man? *Man* being in both can hardly make them equal or the same since one is even *longer* than the other. Again (not to downplay the biblical version of creation in any way – see Jungling, 2007: chapter 3), it is not clear if *man* was subtracted from woman, or *wo*(man) added to *man*. You can take it also to the egg and chicken puzzle, if you like; but could it be because of the inability to understand this type of sameness from the *wo*men that Elton John and others preferred shutting the door on *umogoreys* by *switching* over to the real sameness? Is man-on-man not the real sameness? What might also have provoked the switching over of the *umogoreys* themselves then? Did the men in the factory refuse carrying the heavy load for them "because we are the same"?

These gays and lesbians also confuse heterosexuals enormously.[32] Some heterosexuals just don't know what world they are in (heteronista, homonista, or feminista), hearing two hefty men there, with one calling the other my *wife*! And a woman like Rosie O being called 'my husband' by another woman. Wife and husband indeed who also want their same-sex marriage (SSM) sanctified and legalized! No doubt then that the pro-life movement is ideologically aligned with the anti-SSM movement, being "very powerful in Colorado" (Crehan, 2013: 69), an American state where "Conservative organizations...[like Focus on the Family] are at home in the open political opportunity of U. S. politics" (Crehan, 2013: 70).

Is the SSM husband here based on the KKK-DL of Man-Inside but Woman-Outside and vice versa? If so, was Margaret Mead not right then? I mean when she stated (as cited in Brooks, 1996: 329) that "women may be said to be mothers

---

[32] See, e. g. , Andrew Sullivan, "Why Gay Marriage Is Good for Straight America: As Same-sex Couples March Down the Aisle in New York, the Author Reflects on his own Life, Love, and Pursuit of Happiness" *Newsweek* 158 (2011): 4.

unless they are taught to deny the child-bearing qualities. Society must distort their sense of themselves, pervert their inherent growth-patterns, perpetuate a series of learning outrages upon them, before they will cease to want to provide, at least for a few years, for the child they have already nourished for nine months within the safe circle of their own bodies." As Mindy Barton has demonstrated, Focus on the Family is the primary anti-gay rights organization in Colorado, and is a very large corporation with an expansive direct marketing strategy, compared to relatively small budgets of pro-SSM groups in the state (Crehan, 2013: 70). The really important question is: What is the fuss then when these homosexuals (as same poles not repelling) are also treated differently (from same poles repelling)? Does that not mean that we should treat different things differently?

I am not stepping into that territory right now (having already given a response to it above), except to indicate that the American courts and legislators more than amuse me with the manner they handle the issue of same-sex marriage and other matters revolving thereto (see 'Trojan-Horse-Crazy' below). This whole thing has led Gary Mucciaroni to want to know if it is not clearly the case of same-sex, different politics (Boutcher, 2008). These confused Americans who refuse to learn from anyone else! Some critics cannot understand why, despite public support for anti-discrimination measures in employment for lesbian and gay citizens, as well as scholarly analysis in favour, "even simple anti-discrimination measures are not in force in most U. S. states. While Canada is legalizing same-sex marriage, the U. S. has debated and passed state and federal constitutional amendments to ban same-sex marriages" (Smith, 2005: 227). The 'constitutional amendments' Miriam Smith is talking about include the famous DOMA already seen and its many minis. Shouldn't the confused US of America emulate Canada in this matter?

Letter from Africa To Whiteman: Copying From Copying Canada?

Americans are having a very difficult time imagining how someone could even have posed this question. And they may not be totally wrong being in that bemused state. Canada is not only a Hypocracy; it is also a *Copyocracy*. Call it Copyocratic Hypocracy or Hypocratic Copyocracy, the choice is yours. Be fearless in doing so because (just as Cameroon does to France – see Fossungu, 2013b: chapter 4) Canada is well known for foolishly copying melting-pot America without acknowledgement. For instance, the US of America creates its 'Dancing with the Stars', 'So You Think You Can Dance', etc. and Canada adds Canada to each one of them, etc. Why can't Canada be innovative enough to create its own things out of the blue? It is very simple to explain. Unlike the United States that attracts talents from all over the world and makes competition between them free of residency and citizenship, Canada tricks them in and keeps them out of competition and progress with the residency and citizenship requirements.[33] There are lots of African talents, for example, that would better create uniquely 'multicultural' Canadian TV and other programmes. But they are excluded from exhibiting these talents that should have made Canada truly proud of its being multicultural. How is that done? The exclusion is effected by the very conservative and competition-fearing professional associations. Is the Quebec Bar there? This is only one case. Why has Canada, for instance, never won medals in the sport that Kenyans are noted for in the Olympic Games? Don't tell me that there are no Kenyan-Canadians capable of doing so.

---

[33] "In Chapter One I hazard a description of the essential characteristics of our social and political life [in Canada]: variegated ideology, nationalism, *government presence and lack of competition in the economy*, deference to authority and hierarchy, regionalism, the English and the French" (Bogart, 1994: x, emphasis added).

They are there in their multitude, but they do not get to be selected to represent the country for reasons you and I already know.

Canadian Experience My Foot!

My one foot is more than enough. But I will prefer to give you not just one of my feet here but the two since they are not all *pietinering* the same trashy stuff. One is standing on the shortage of medical doctors while the other on some other doctors lecturing in Windsor and creating a doctor deficiency too.

The Medical Doctors Shortage Hypocracy

I know a Burundian professional in MYR, for example. This is a professional that my French-speaking friends would say *"travail là où les autres s'amusent."* I am talking about a gynaecologist. Why do you think Dr Kuba (with several years of professional practice in Burundi) is in the forest cutting trees rather than working in a clinic or hospital in town? Because Health Canada and other institutions would tell you that he has no "Canadian Experience". Canadian experience indeed! So when is he ever going to get that until he is employed somewhere in Canada as the professional that he has been trained to be? Hypocratic Roundaboutism!

For my PAB (*préposé aux bénéficiares*) *stage* in 2010, I was assigned to a Maison des Aînés in Côte-Saint-Luc. As a shift partner I had this Asian lady from Pakistan. She just couldn't stand the food being served to the *bénéficiares* or clients (perhaps because of pork presence?). We therefore had our deal – she led in the cleaning and bathing of the clients who were mostly females and I took the wheel in feeding them. She was so grateful. I always kept speculating on why and how she chose the profession when she had the food 'allergies'? One day I decided to wonder aloud to her. "Colleague," she wondered back, "do I really have a choice?" What do you mean? I asked, looking forward to enlightenment. She had trained in Pakistan as a medical doctor (paediatrician, to be precise). After some years of practice there, she immigrated to Canada. Until our discussion, Dr Malik had tried to no avail to get into the profession, for reasons we already know by now. Yet, every day we hear on Canadian radio and TV how there is severe shortage of doctors in Canada!

The Windsor Lecturers Road-Blocking Schemes

It is also like the University of Windsor complaining of the dearth of lecturers and, therefore, having graduate and undergraduates always sitting in the same class for almost all the courses. Yet, the same people concerned would be doing everything in their power to prevent very capable African students from ever reaching the lecturer rank. Unlike the Lockwood Manufacturing antagonistic environment (see Fossungu, 2014b: 46-47), the university is supposed to be a place where you would expect level-headedness and objectivity. Not so in some Canadian universities, with the University of Windsor exemplifying here. I got into the M. A. in Political Science programme in Windsor last year and was doing well (my trademark too) until my first write-up in the three lecturers' courses of the first semester. Of course, I would not write a paper and use material or ideas from previous publications without referencing that. For instance, in addressing the multiple questions posed,[34] I stated somewhere in my 20-page paper that:

Stoker and Marsh (2010: 8) quickly indicate therefore that the alarm bells might be ringing here since it appears that political scientists cannot even agree what the subject matter of their discipline should be, submitting though that both arena

---

[34] 'How have different approaches in political science answered the question of what is politics, and what is an appropriately scientific approach to the study of politics? What divisions, overlaps, challenges, and/or opportunities for political scientists are presented by different and competing responses to these questions?'

and process definitions have their value and could accommodate themselves to much shared ground on the issue of what the political is. Thus, there are repeated and clear calls for celebration of diversity in political science by Stoker and Marsh (2010: 1, 6, 11-12) and Hay (2013). These advocacies could be very sensible in that participants in an academic discussion must "Not Agree[] Just to Avoid Disagreement" (Fossungu, 2013: 60-62).

Here is what the lecturer writes against this passage in the course of his grading: "What's the [] in the middle here? Also, you've clearly written and published a lot before. I keep wondering why you're back in an MA program given you already have the legal scholarship and degrees. Are the degrees not recognized in Canada (which is itself, of course a major problem)? Anyway, we can talk about that later outside of class." Yeah, Canadian degrees not recognized in Canada! Another of the three lecturers said to me when I went to her/his office for some clarifications: "I hear you have a Ph. D.?" I said yes and s/he demanded what area my doctorate is in. My response was "I am sure whoever told you I have a Ph. D. must also have indicated in what discipline." It is not even like my admission to the MA programme was done without knowledge that I was already holder of multiple Canadian Master's degrees and a doctorate. Some of the said lecturers' collective war was on and they devised the strategy of giving me close to failure grades. I have seen this story before, of course, in McGill (see Fossungu, 2013a: 67-68). According to them, then, referencing my own work in the papers was my way of showing-up or bragging? Of course, that is not it. Otherwise, would the reviewers of this book (as well as of my other works) not also be saying the same, in view of the copious references to my earlier works? Is that the way it works?

Of course, that is again not it. They just wanted me not to do so, so that they could validly cry plagiarism in the same way

136

as the MYR *contremaître* attempted to lure me into the '*réprise*' circle. This MYR *contremaître* thought that, because I was a newcomer and (Black) African, he could play his routine moutonization-inspired pranks on me too. He came to my very first patch and, rather than congratulating me for doing an excellent job, was instead urging me to do a bad job (hurry) in order to make the money. Don't forget that he will be the first to turn around and recommend *réprise* of the patch when I would have declared its completion. How is redoing the patch for a day or two going to aid me in making money? And when (as a newcomer) you start with *réprise*, be sure to be a regular customer or victim. I therefore went into my trademark question-and-answer session with him. "Who owns this patch or *térrain?*" You, he said. So, I am the *master* of this patch, right? "Yes." I understand then what you are up to, I told him. "I am not a master of the French language. But the meaning of your title I know too well. Your job is to be against the *master* of the patch. Were it otherwise, why would you be *encouraging* me to make money unless you truly want me not to make money?" He left me alone, walking away like someone who had mistaken his route. Is that any different from the Windsor lecturers' attitude? Imagine me then, after the Windsor M. A. program, applying for an advertised position at the Department of Political Science and sitting in front of these same doctors for an interview! Not this me at all. If it is only in Windsor, then I say that I already have a job that I love very much – writing about my rare life experiences that do not include the "Canadian experience" that the copyocrats are fond of blocking African intellectuals and other professionals with. I am unquestionably unstoppable.

But that does not give anyone the right to want to prevent people from getting to their destinations. This is such a headache for many others such as my African colleagues. One of them intended to proceed to do a doctorate. I used to think that writing a thesis/dissertation was a given for Master's and

Ph. D. programmes until I got to Windsor. That is, that the Master's with or without thesis depended on the candidate's choice, not the institution selecting those who can write a thesis or not. Add to that the fact that this African scholar that everyone in class knows to be so good at contributing ideas to the discussions would get a *seventy-something* as participation marks while a white undergraduate student who has been clearly absent for two weeks gets a *ninety-five*! Even the white student was really surprised that she had those marks in view of what said African (of all) had. It is quite an overlong tale. Brief, the whole strategy was just to make sure that the African's chances of getting to the Ph. D. level are practically zero, notwithstanding that the said African is a Canadian permanent resident.

The American Trojan-Horse-Crazy or the Comforting Deception of Religion?

Because the 'residence/citizenship' card can't apply to people like said African and me, we would thus observably be told that there are better *experienced* people for doing the copying from down south. These Canadian-experienced 'professionals' even do the copying without considering us Quebecers who eventually have to go about creating our own French-only versions of programmes like "Stars Academie", etc. Where then is the national unity that comes with a true sense of belonging with others? Of course, no one is equating uniformization with unity here (see Fossungu, 2013b; 2013c). But it is amazing that when it is time for a Quebec referendum vote the copyocrats in Ottawa would shamelessly ferry people into *La Belle Province* to tell us: "Quebec we love you!" Are they here not just mistakenly putting in 'Quebec' instead of 'America'? Get the message clear and let it sink well into the skulls. Just don't wait until there is a referendum here to come telling or showing us that we are loved, and merit being part and parcel of Canada; a country which is now being credited with having something at least (on gay and lesbian rights) worth copying by the Americans?

Putnam and Campbell (2012: 36) while praising American religious harmony would nevertheless agree "that abortion and homosexuality have come to be especially salient in contemporary politics, which in turn has led to a religious divide at the ballot box" (2012: 22; also Patrikios, 2008). This division over said issues cuts across several spectrums and levels, including regions of the country. Thus, in Margaret Gram Crehan's *The Divided States of America* on the same-sex issue, she makes the states' political and legal response to the issue of same-sex marriage the dependent variable, with the independent variables being the states' political cultures, the networks of interest groups for and against same-sex marriage, and their different law making processes. The key questions that motivated her research are: What factors would account for the legal and political responses to same-sex marriage issue particularly in California, Colorado and Massachusetts? What factors usually influence the strategic path taken by key interest groups on the issue of same-sex marriage? (Crehan, 2013: 7-9).

The SSM (same-sex marriage) is a phenomenon that Mariam Smith and others have scathingly defined as the quintessential "values" issue in American politics. In support of the description, the critics point out that in the 2004 presidential elections eleven states banned gay marriage and the marriage ban referenda were credited with increasing voting turnout in some states (Smith, 2005: 225; Patrikios, 2008; Crehen, 2013). Although the issue of marriage equality is the same across the United States, it "is not nearly as widespread as it is in Canada" (Smith, 2005: 225). Boutcher would contend that even such "marriage equality has yet to have widespread success" (2010: 1503). Granted that it even is, Margaret Gram Crehan sees the outcome, on the other hand, being vastly different from state to state not to mention the federal government. She wonders about what could account for the different paths states have taken when it comes to recognizing or banning same-sex marriage; why some states have granted full marriage benefits to same-sex couples, some have passed constitutional amendments (known as mini-DOMAs) banning same-sex marriage, and others have provided civil unions, which allot certain rights, but not full marriage rights, to same-sex couples (Crehan, 2013: 3). As noted previously, Canada has legalized SSM. Would these Americans not be humble enough to emulate Canada then? No way! Only over our dead bodies, Uncle Sam's children have federally said.[35]

Yet, the same American government would be pressurizing African governments to legalize homosexuality which the latter find to be contrary to their customs. Is this hypocrisy or David Wexelblat's (2012) 'Trojan Horse'? As Canada has already owned the first, why doesn't the US just content itself with Trojan-Horse-Crazy? The recent controversy over homosexuality particularly in Uganda has brought anti-gay groups into existence around the continent, as epitomized by this email to 'Whiteman' being circulated by one of these groups from Ghana:

Dear whiteman,

You asked us to wear coat under hot sun, we did; you said we should speak your language, we have obediently ignored ours. You asked us to tie a rope round our necks like goats, we have obeyed without questioning. You asked our ladies to wear dead people's hair instead of the natural ones God gave to them, they have obeyed. You said we should marry just one

---

[35] For further analysis of the stiff constitutional and other problems confronting the American federal government in the matter of legalizing or banning same-sex marriage across the country, see Peter Ateh-Afac Fossungu, "Religion, Same-Sex Marriage, and the Courts in American Politics" (Major Research Paper for the Award of Master of Arts – Political Science, defended on December 23, 2014, University of Windsor)

woman in the midst of plenty damsels, we reluctantly agreed. You said our decent girls should wear catapults instead of the conventional pants, they have obeyed. You asked us to use rubber in order to control our birth rate, we agreed though it denies us of the sweetness of SEX. Now you want our MEN to sleep with fellow MEN and our WOMEN with fellow WOMEN so that God would visit us like Sodom and Gomora? White folk, we say tufiakwa!!! Na by force to be your friend? we no go gree with you this time. As proud Ghanaians, we say a huge NO to GAY relationships.

Anti-gay groups of Ghana,

Signed by the secretary Ghanaba Kwabena Amansie to the western world.

The Arab world is partly African and therefore also part of said anti-gay groups that the continent is sprouting up.[36] We have already discussed most of these things but two broad issues will now be employed to bring out the comforting deceptions of religion: (1) Tessierizing the Sensational Narratives and (2) Marriage as a Religious Sacrament/Right.

Tessierizing the Sensational Narratives
In a volume dedicated "To the innocent victims of conflict in the Middle East" (Saikal and Schnabel, 2003: vii), what Schnabel (2003: 1-22) sees as "A rough journey [in the] Nascent democratization in the Middle East" would largely explain the persistence of authoritarianism in the region, prior to, and perhaps even after, the recent shakeups of late 2010 and early 2011.[37] The edited volume, *Religion, Democracy and*

---

[36] South Africa is a special case since it has legalized homosexuality. See its 2006 Constitution's Chapter 2, Section 9(3). For more extensive discussion of this country's position, see Thoreson (2013).

[37] These shakeups would constitute what Dabashi (2012) and Ross (2011) call 'The Arab Spring', what others like Haddad, Bsheer and Abu-

Politics in the Middle East, highlights and discusses the "five dilemmas or challenges [the Arab Spring poses] for those seeking to understand the region" (Byman, 2012a: vii-xi). Most of these dilemmas/challenges are (1) Consistency versus Oversimplification, (2) Reality versus Perception, (3) Dominance of Islamism, (4) The Internal Dynamics of the Peace Process, and (5) Weakness of States and Uncertainty. Like Byman (2012a), Dabashi has also provided an in-depth analysis of most of these same narratives that are meant for "The Manipulation of [Effective] Political Opposition" (Lust-Okar, 2005: 22-35). Dabashi does so in his chapter 6 titled 'The Centre Cannot Hold' (Dabashi, 2012: 141-54), wherein he handles them under the following five headings: Who is History's Master?; The East is West, the West is East; False Anxieties; The Islamic Republic in Bahrain; and Decolonizing a World.

To properly understand the implications of the Arab Spring, it would be appropriate to take a further brief but intertwined view of the religious/cultural argument literature. There are many studies in the domain but the better place to begin is probably Mark Tessier's 2002 study which examined the influence of Islam on attitudes toward democracy using public opinion data collected in Palestine (West Bank and Gaza), Morocco, Algeria, and Egypt. In surveys conducted by or in collaboration with Arab scholars, interview schedules containing questions about governance and democracy and also about conceptions and practices relating to Islam were administered to comparatively large and representative samples of adults in all four countries, including two samples in Egypt. These data provide a strong empirical foundation from which to address questions about the relationship between Islam and democracy at the individual level of analysis (Tessier, 2002:

Rish (2012) brand as 'The Arab Uprisings', and what Alhassen and Shihab-Eldin (2012) term 'The Arab Revolutions'.

337). He was motivated to carry out this project because he had found out that answers to the issue of whether or not Islam inhibits democracy in the Arab world "are most often based on impressionistic and anecdotal information… influenced by western stereotypes about Arabs and Muslims" (2002: 337) By contrast, he notes, systematic empirical inquiries into the nature, distribution, and determinants of political attitudes in the Arab world are rare (Tessier, 2002: 337). This absence or scarcity of relevant scholarship has been attributed to the neglect of the region in the 1980s and 1990s by experts of comparative politics. Posusney (2004: 127) has clearly indicated that scholarly work on the Middle East has since the 80s been marginalized within the study of developing countries and, even more, in the broader field of comparative politics.

Thus, many studies would suggest that factors which differentiate the Arab world from the U. S, and Europe may be of limited importance so far as the influence of religion on political attitudes is concerned (Tessier, 2002: 349; Putnam and Campbell, 2012; Campbell and Putnam, 2012). Moreover, even in regard of the U. K. and U. S. which are considered as 'most similar' by the 'Most similar'-and-'most different' theory (see Hopkin, 2010: 292-93), "there are so many potentially relevant differences between the two countries" (Hopkin, 2010: 293). Undermining the simplistic view of religion in the Arab world is also the blind eye given to the question of reform within Islam – a struggle for the soul of Islam (Esposito, 2012: 162-65). Most Muslims in the Arab world strongly identify with Islam, but they disagree as to its proper role in government, law, and society, as well as over vexing questions such as the role of women in a Muslim society and the rights of religious minorities (Esposito, 2012: 169-173, 182-84). Of course, these issues and differences over them are not unique to only Muslim societies. Women only got the right to vote (for instance) in most western democracies in recent years, and we know from the discussion so far that the discipline of political science itself

143

is mainly still a male-dominated area in most western universities.

Indeed, Byman (2012a: ix) has even found that the differences within the Islamist community often dwarf those between Islamists and more-secular forces; with Hasan (2007: 24) positing that the "Islamic Republic of Iran provides a very complex case for any assessment of democracy and human rights." Iran adheres officially to Islam (see Zibakalam, 2007; Saikal, 2003). As such, it is assumed by Western scholars that the regime must be oppressive. This is what Said (2001) qualifies as "an exhibition of ignorance" of "a clumsy writer and inelegant thinker." And he could be quite right because the historical picture is much more complex. Informed studies have shown that, far from the monolithic, totalitarian police state described by some commentators, Iran's politics reflects an intensely complex, highly plural, dynamic characteristic of a state in transition that incorporates the contradictions and instabilities inherent in such a process (Hasan, 2007: 24; Saikal, 2003: 169-176).

Available data from Tessier's work would suggest, moreover, that religion influences political orientations more frequently and consistently in the West than in the Arab world (see, for America, Putnam and Campbell, 2012; Black *et al*, 2011); with the evidence presently available from Palestine, Morocco, Algeria, and Egypt suggesting that Islam is not the obstacle to democratization that some western and other scholars allege it to be. A democratic, civic, and participatory political culture may be necessary for mature democracy, but Tessier's study suggests that only to a very limited extent is the emergence of such a political culture discouraged by the Islamic attachments of ordinary Arab citizens (Tessier, 2002: 350). A detailed analysis of the requirements for democratic transition can be found in Schnabel (2003); Najem (2003); Owen (2000); Lust-Okar (2005); Byman (2012b); and Tessier (2002: 338-39).

From the foregoing analysis, one can reach the conclusion that, with the Arab Spring clearly exposing the constructed 'reality', and being therefore a real threat to 'The Centre That Can No Longer Hold', new narratives (such as Playing the Iran and Muslim Brotherhood Cards) must have to be speedily erected and fortified. The whole idea seems to be that of making sure that power in the Arab world is kept away from anyone who is judged by the West as incapable of 'Selling the Sea to Stay in Power'. Such a person clearly would not furnish an effective camouflage or blanket for "the wanton disregard practised by neoliberal predatory capitalism" (Dabashi, 2012: 62) which Shaddiq Al-Jawi finds to be 'in sharp conflict with the freedoms found in Islam'. We have already heard clearly from Raymond Baker about 'the West', championed by the USA, seeing Islam as a formidable stumbling block to their hegemonic and homogenizing agenda, a programme that is also facing challenge on the home front.

Marriage As A Religious Sacrament/Right: To Belong Or Not To Belong, That Is The Question?

It is also true to say that the West is not a cartoonlike world, since not everyone there is in support of or against certain values, including same-sex unions. DeLaet and Caufield (2008: 320) also see the conservative's support of state-imposed sectarian definitions of marriage as representing an inconsistency. Crehan (2013) sees the confusion as dividing the states of America. DeLaet and Caufield question to know why religious liberty shouldn't protect the right of mainline American religious communities to sanctify same-sex unions as they see fit and to have such recognitions given the same legal status as marriages blessed by other churches. In this context, these brilliant authors say, we must ask ourselves—religious conservatives, religious liberals, and the non-religious alike— what religious liberty means. They think that a religious rights framework applied to the issue of gay marriage suggests that the American government violates disestablishment norms when it endorses a sectarian definition of marriage. In doing so, the government is promoting a very selective form of religious liberty indeed (DeLaet and Caufield, 2008: 320). All this shows, as a critic put it in 1992, that religion, like all ideologies, can act to change society, or to preserve the status quo (Westley, 1992: 349). Westley's reflection that opens this chapter could greatly help our understanding of the dynamics behind the struggle for same-sex marriage in the United States particularly and the world at large.

Katherine E. Knutson thinks the religious dimension of debates over abortion and same-sex marriage has received much media attention in recent years, whereas the issues in which religious groups take interest are varied and have shifted over time. Some policy debates, she explains, focus on issues that affect religious belief or practice directly while others concern policies that religious groups or individuals care about as a result of religious beliefs (Knutson, 2011: 359). Even if the same-sex Hypocratic solution is copied from us Canadians, America would still be bedevilled by yet another conundrum hinging on colour or race – the theorization about which has led to suggestions that some priests are surely not going to like imagining – that Adam and Eve were Blacks. If Americans truly want to frankly handle these SSM problems, they would do so without even looking up north where the question of marriage as a religious sacrament still remains thorny for the Catholics and their unmarried priests. This section first examines this other oddity with Catholics whose priests do not partake in the sacrament of marriage before looking further at the battle for SSM as a legal/religious right.

Catholicism Equals Inconsistencies?
Catholics, like most Christian denominations, would preach that there are seven sacraments, one of which is marriage. Yet,

the catholic preacher must not marry? It just does not make sense especially when we consider that the Bible itself says God told his creations, human beings especially, to go forth and be fruitful and multiply. It is not clear why the Vatican can continue to hang on to this contradiction even when we are well aware of the passage opening chapter 2 of this book, namely, that marriage is for the purpose of procreation. Just hear their justification against the decision of the 2003 Massachusetts case known as *Goodridge v. Department of Public Health* that recognises the right of same-sex couples to marry and you will quickly and completely agree with Cunningham (2005: 21-22) that "The [Catholic] Church is from Mars, the Court is from Venus."

In connection with the multiple challenges facing the institution of marriage that we have noted above (especially in chapter 2), the non-Catholic Christian churches have attempted getting involved in the hope of advising couples through means such as marriage counselling. The big question becomes that of how the local Catholic Church, which is headed by the unmarried priest, is going to correctly do so without some personal knowledge of how it feels to be married? This query is appropriate if you consider these other question that Westbrook ((2010: 4-5) has gone on to ask: What about the role of local churches? Have local congregations or their ministers turned their backs on the institution of marriage? How effective have ministers and local churches been in this area of ministry? How important is marriage to local churches? How important are local churches to marriages? How important are local churches to the institution of marriage? Have local churches contributed to the decline of marriage in North America? In an era of mega-churches, rampant church planting, and the widespread decline of many "traditional" churches, where does marriage stand?

The purpose of Neil Westbrook's research project then was to examine these and similar questions by studying the role of the local church as it relates to the institution of marriage. Much of the scholarly research on this critically important topic, he asserted, has not included what the church is or should be doing. He goes on to indicate that in recent years some churches have implemented pre-marital counselling programs to try to address some of the shortcomings of marriage among congregants. Others have offered marriage enrichment retreats as a way to offer support to married couples and strengthen marriages. Any approach, however, Westbrook concludes, *should have a clear understanding of the problems and challenges associated with marriage and the role of the local church before it can begin to propose remedial or enrichment strategies that address the issues and problems of marriage today* (2010:5, my emphasis). Neil Westbrook is right on top of the issues here.

As I have questioned earlier, how is the unmarried priest going to get a good handle on the problems of marriage? An answer or something like it appears to be coming from Peter Acho Awoh who in 2012 undertook a fascinating study of Christian enclaves in the Southern Cameroons of the colonial era (*The Residue of the Western Missionary in the Southern Cameroons*). The Christian enclaves came into being with absolute spontaneity as a modus vivendi. However what had taken root in the territory as a self-protection mechanism, soon unleashed its lethal, enticing tentacles luring both the wives of royals and commoners into their bosom. This disruptive influence of Christian villages threatened the survival of ethnic groups, arousing the rancour of traditional authorities and civil administrators.[38] It is then not surprising that C. S. Lewis is cited by Westbrook (2010: 2) for saying that "My own view is that the Churches should frankly recognize that the majority of the British people are not Christians and, therefore, cannot be expected to live Christian lives."

---

[38] See http://www. langaa-rpcig. net/The-Residue-of-the-Western. html.

Corroboration may come again from Awoh who goes on to indicate how in many ways the Christian enclaves inhibited the potential of colonial governments to administer the territory. These states within a state (like the Vatican is) propagated by the missionary in the most insidious and perfidious of all manners sowed within their own bosom the seed of self-destruction. The whole issue of runaway wives of royals and commoners alike who took refuge in the Christian villages troubled both the colonial and traditional authorities. By offering a safe haven to these runaway wives and welcoming women who were outside the traditional male authority in a tribal setup, the missionaries began sowing within the Christian communities the seeds of their own self destruction. Records of wives of Fons and commoners escaping into these enclaves, eloping with a man and returning pregnant remained the regular subject of several colonial intelligence reports. Highhanded methods by missionaries in these villages brought both the missionaries and their work into disrepute. In less than a quarter of a century these enclaves had lost the war of attrition waged by colonial and traditional authorities. Worn out by endless strife and dissension within and without and forced by contingency, what had been conceived to be ideal Christian communities with snowballing effects, saw its premature demise.[39]

The Priesty-Boy Thesis: If what Awoh has said is not clear enough on the fornicating 'men of god', then just leave your *NOSIFE* (no schooling in four-eyesism) again and follow me into the *HISOFE* (Higher School of Four-Eyesism) as we examine the sexual drive function of marriage. Discussing the purposes of marriage, Laurie A. Jungling tells us that there are three principally. If I may be permitted to repeat for better understanding, first, marriage is for procreation and

---

[39] See http://www. langaa-rpcig. net/The-Residue-of-the-Western. html.

149

propagation of the human race; explaining why, for Martin Luther who broke ranks with the Catholics, marriage was not just a matter of creating children, but also nourishing them and raising them to be godly adults who fulfil their proper roles in society. Luther insisted that the family, with the marital relation at the centre, was the foundation for all social order (Jungling, 2007: 68). The second purpose for marriage was the social purpose, through which men and women fulfilled their roles in and for society so that order and peace could be maintained. Thirdly, marriage is for the control and channelling of the sex drive. Contrary to some of his contemporaries (notably the Catholics), Jungling concludes, Luther believed that the sex drive in humans was a natural thing created by God for the purpose of procreation (2007: 68-69). Over to Catholics to tell us how their priests fit into all of these roles of this important sacrament. How do the priests control and channel their sex drives?

Are Africans still in doubt regarding how the comforting deceptions of religion in this respect are often carried out? Yeah! African priests have for too long been dreaming, stupidly tying and hanging up their *mblacauses* to dry up uselessly. It is not until recently that they have realized that most of these white priests that are sent to confuse and abuse Africans have either already made their families in their home countries or/and are simply fornicators/homosexuals who are simply looking for a haven where they can practise their child/wife abuse and sodomy without detection and punishment. Dr Paul Cameron of the Family Research Institute defines homosexuals "as perpetrators of child sexual abuse who also have reduced life expectations."[40] They therefore want to make the 'best' of their short twisted lives! This theory is sort of reflected in the

---

[40]Cited in Crehan, 2013: 71. See also Phil Lawler, "Homosexual Network at the Vatican, Yes; Reason for the Pope's Resignation, No" February 22, 2013, available @ http://www. catholicculture. org/commentary/otn. cfm?id=968.

Priesty-Boy Tale from Stephen Ajab Asong's '*Breaking News*' that was sent to the CGAM Forum on June 29, 2009:

A woman has an affair during the day while her husband is at work.

Her nine-year-old son comes home unexpectedly, sees the illegal lovers and hides in the bedroom cupboard to watch. Then the woman's husband unexpectedly comes home.

She hides her lover in the cupboard, not realizing that her little boy is in there already.

The little Boy says: 'Dark in here. '

The Man says: 'Yes, it is. '

Boy: 'I have a soccer ball, do you want to buy it?'

Man: 'No, thanks. '

Boy: 'My dad's outside, I'll call him if you don't buy it!'

Man: 'OK, how much?'

Boy: '$150'

A few weeks later it happened again and the boy and the lover were in the cupboard together again.

Boy: 'Dark in here'.

Man: 'Yes, it is. '

Boy: 'I have soccer boots. '

The Man, remembering the last time, asks the boy 'How much?'

The Boy says:'$350'

The Man says: 'Fine, I will buy them. '

A few days later, the Father says to the boy: 'Grab your ball and boots, let's go outside and have a game. '

The Boy says: 'I can't, I sold them for $500. '

The Father says: 'That's terrible to over-charge your friends like that. . . $500 is way more than those two things cost. I'm going to take you to church and make you confess your sins. 'They go to church and the father makes the little boy sit in the confession booth and he closes the door.

The Boy says: 'Dark in here. '

The Priest says: 'Don't start that sh!t again!'
THIS IS MY CHURCH NOT YOUR FATHER'S HOUSE!!!

Oh these so-called 'Men of God' and their 'Satanic Deeds'! Hear any of them in the pulpit sermonizing against homosexuality[41] and foolishly devoted Africans (who are out there saying NO to Gay relationships) would hardly believe you if you tell them their preacher is one clear gay. Once more, I say Africans and other 'uncivilized' peoples of the world had better be 'civilization-savvy' with these wolves in goat skins. One would prefer to deal with openly gay officials like Colorado State Senator Pat Steadman and State Representative Mark Ferrandino who, in February 2011, "brought forward a Civil Union Bill" addressing "financial responsibility of partners, medical decision-making and treatment, inheritance, ability to designate a partner as retirement beneficiary, ability to adopt the child of one's partner, insurance of partner, family leave benefits, responsibility of conservator, guardian, or personal representative" (Crehen, 2013: 71).

Battling Same-Sex Marriage As A Religious Right?

Most Africans are surely going to regard this topic as a clean case of WONDERS SHALL NEVER END. Some commentators think that the question of where to begin in the analysis of the struggle over same-sex marriage in the US is difficult. This difficulty, I think, could be exacerbated by what I theorized on above as the Ku Klux Klan Dubious-Logic (KKK-DL), since until the coming out of the closet by some big names (stars like Elton John, Ellen D etc.) one could never

---

[41] See, for instance, Cunningham (2005); "Vatican Set to Fight Gay Marriages: Alarmed by Legal Acceptance of Same-sex Unions, Set to Launch Global Campaign to Rally Opposition" *Toronto Star* (27 Aug, 2003), A04; "Same-sex Marriage Minister Punished" 129:9 *The Presbyterian Record* (Oct 2005) 16; and "Anti-gay Protester Convicted: Woman Shoved Cleric before Same-sex Marriage Ceremony, Appeal Court Rules that Attack in Church More than a Trifle" *Toronto Star* (29 July, 2004), B05.

have known who was or was not a gay/lesbian. But Crehen, (2013: 13-14) thinks the discussion could begin with *Baker v. Nelson* in 1971, when Jack Baker and Mike McConnell attempted to marry in Minnesota under the theory that since there was no specific prohibition against same-sex marriage, the legislature must have intended to allow it. Baker and McConnell were denied a marriage license based on the fact that they were the same sex. They first brought suit in a lower Minnesota court claiming that the Minnesota Statute did not specifically require that the applicants be of different sexes. They also argued that if the Court found that the statute did have this intent, then it violated the First Amendment's freedom of speech and association, the Eighth Amendment's prohibition against cruel and unusual punishment, the Ninth Amendment's un-enumerated right to privacy and the Fourteenth Amendment because there was a fundamental right to marry under the Due Process Clause and sex discrimination is contrary to the Equal Protection Clause.

Because religious actors have been a driving force behind opposition to gay marriage, it seems counter-intuitive to argue that gay marriage can be considered a religious right (DeLaet and Caufield, 2008: 298). However, religious actors in the United States do not speak with one voice, as, interestingly, seven of the fourteen plaintiffs in the 2003 *Goodridge* case were Unitarian Universalists (DeLaet and Caufield, 2008: 299). The many other examples of various congregations that have been performing wedding ceremonies for same-sex couples for several years now do specifically sustain the fact that "gay marriage can be considered a fundamental religious right derived from First Amendment guarantees of religious liberty and non-establishment of religion" (DeLaet and Caufield, 2008: 298). Debra DeLaet and Rachel Caufield believe this is a better course to tread because:

A religious rights frame for the debate over gay marriage suggests that the federal and state governments inappropriately violate the Religion Clauses of the First Amendment with marriage licensing and benefits policies that give preferential status to heterosexual unions sanctified in religious ceremonies but deny the same recognition and rights to same-sex unions, even those that are blessed by churches that support gay marriage. In particular, such discriminatory practices violate the "neutrality principle" by privileging a religious conception of marriage favored by some religious traditions but not universally shared by all mainline religions. In this regard, it is important to note that religious conservatives have been the driving force behind the movement to define marriage as a union between a man and a woman, and this definition of marriage is unquestionably shaped by sectarian, religious beliefs [DeLaet and Caufield, 2008: 300].

Furnishing an incredible amount of legal precedent for gay marriage as a religious right (DeLaet and Caufield, 2008: 308-314), these authors theorize that "the fact that a religious rights framework has not gained traction in the debate over abortion does not necessarily diminish its potential for advancing marriage equality for same-sex couples" (DeLaet and Caufield, 2008: 305). Debra DeLaet and Rachel Caufield could be making a lot of sense here. The plaintiffs' lengthy list in *Baker v. Nelson* would seem to show to me that they were unaware of Jay Sekulow ("a nice Jewish boy from Brooklyn" – Toobin, 2011: 325) who successfully shifted gears completely away from heavily relying on the Free Exercise Clauses to simply Free Expression/Speech with religious cases. In other words, Sekulow developed the legal strategy of defending religious expression cases as free speech cases (Black *et al*, 2011: 312). He did so through cases such as *Board of Airport Commissioners of the City of Los Angeles v. Jews for Jesus Inc.* (1987), and *Board of*

Education of Westside Community Schools v. Mergens, both cases discussed by Toobin (2011: 325-327), because he found a receptive audience in the Supreme Court, wining every time he appeared in the Supreme Court (Black *et al*, 2011: 312). The Minnesota litigants should have known better to go for the services of an 'old hand' because in judicial decision making, particularly in religion cases, not all attorneys are equal; with experienced lawyers enjoying an advantage over their colleagues who have not participated as frequently in litigation (Wahlbeck, 2011: 317).

Thus, in line with Jay Sekulow or someone like him, most critics think that framing gay marriage as a religious right suggests that the parties who are harmed by marriage laws discriminating against same-sex couples include not only the individual men and women in these relationships but also the churches who support gay marriage and their members, regardless of their sexual orientation (DeLaet and Caufield 2008: 300). This reasoning seems to ring a lot of bells, being seemingly analogous to Sekulow's in *Lamb's Chapel v. Center Moriches Union Free School District* where he argued that "[t]his is the type of viewpoint discrimination that this Court has not sanctioned" (Toobin, 2011: 327).

Absent Jay Sekulow or someone like him, the Minnesota trial court dismissed the claims of the plaintiffs in *Baker v. Nelson* and the same-sex couple appealed to the Minnesota Supreme Court. The Minnesota Supreme Court first examined the statute itself and the common usage of the term "marriage" and found that other references were gender-specific and thus the statute did prohibit marriage between persons of the same-sex. But the Court distinguished the proffered marriage cases (like *Loving v. Virginia* in 1967), finding that there is a clear distinction between a marital restriction based on race and one based on the fundamental difference in sex. Baker's petition for a writ of certiorari from the U. S. Supreme Court was denied for failure to present a federal question (Crehan, 2013:

14). Clearly, this decision or legal dictum is telling us that marriage issues are the states' jurisdiction, not for the federal government. But the question relates to whether the courts always follow their own judgments. That is, do they follow *stare decisis* which Wahlbeck (2011: 321) says is "[t]he principal norm of the American legal system"?

The last question is very crucial because, although regulation of marriage in the United States has traditionally been left up to the states, the federal government in 1996 responded to state court decisions favourable to same-sex marriage (Crehan, 2013: 13)by going ahead and passing the DOMA, which we have already seen above defining marriage as the legal union between one man and one woman as man and wife, leading to a revival of "[t]he ideological battles over the values of the new nation [that] were waged in statehouses, churches, and in the press" (McGarvie, 2000: iv). As some critics have pointed out clearly, this legislation was passed by an overwhelming majority in Congress (three hundred and forty-two to sixty-seven in the House and eighty-five to fourteen in the Senate) and was signed into law by President Bill Clinton. Owing to what they view as an aggressive judicial assault on traditional marriage, religious conservatives have sought to enshrine this definition more absolutely in the legal fabric of the United States political system by advocating for the Federal Marriage Amendment, which would constitutionally define marriage as a legal union between one man and one woman (DeLaet and Caufield, 2008: 305). This categorization is one "as generally understood in the western, Judeo-Christian tradition. It does not refer to or include gay marriage, common law marriage or cohabitation" (Westbrook, 2010: 6). With that sort of definition, 'the gloves were off', if I may borrow from Hamid Dabashi here.

Some commentators do think the definition is not what is in question because gays and lesbians, who have for the most part been raised by heterosexual parents, know exactly what marriage is – and they want to be in. To these analysts, the fight is rather over *which couples* get to belong to this institution (Crehan, 2013: 7). Margaret Gram Crehan wonders nevertheless why anyone would want to belong to an institution where some do not want them as a member. Citing Groucho Marx who said "I don't want to belong to any club that will accept me as a member", Crehan explains that the quote is meant to caution the reader that marriage is not the ultimate goal of the gay rights movement, nor should it be, because marriage will not set gays and lesbians free – free from the discrimination they face on a daily basis, free from being targets of hate crimes, free from having to pay for benefits that are available to married heterosexual couples (Crehan, 2013: 7; Thoreson, 2013: 646-49). Some critics would seem to agree here that the Canadian situation is more advanced than the American when they theorize that despite that the courts have issued rulings in favour of same-sex marriage in Hawaii (*Baehr v. Lewin*), Vermont, and Massachusetts (*Goodridge*), "political mobilization in support of lesbian and gay rights faces well-organized and well-entrenched opposition and seems unlikely to succeed in the foreseeable future" (Smith, 2005: 225).

Some recent events would appear to both prove and disprove these 2005 critics. Clear examples include the recent March 2014 beer brewery controversy in Boston's St. Patrick Day Parade, resulting from exclusions of gay veterans from participation. A local gay pub announced its stoppage of selling the brewery's beer because of its decades-long sponsorship of the parade that discriminates against homosexuals. Not only the brewery but also City Hall then threatened not to participate in the parade if it was not open to all without discrimination. While some would see this as victory, others would not.

To shed light on the variety of ways states have handled this issue Margaret Crehan has therefore conducted a comparative case study of three states: Colorado,

Massachusetts and California. Each of them has taken vastly different actions on the issue of same-sex marriage. For example, Colorado has a DOMA which acts as a same-sex marriage ban. Massachusetts was the first state to allow same-sex marriage and has issued over 11,000 such licenses, and lastly, California is perhaps the most complicated, having gone from issuing same-sex marriage licenses to passing Prop 8 which banned same-sex marriage, and then, after a United States Supreme Court ruling, the state once again began issuing same-sex marriage licenses (Crehan, 2013: 8). Such conflicting stances appear to give credence to Karl Marx's thesis (cited in Westley, 1992: 346) that "Religion is the sigh of the oppressed creature, the sentiment of a heartless world and the soulless conditions. It is the opium of the people." Crehan chose to study those three states also because they represent different geographical locations of the United States, they have different political cultures as indicated by the parties that control state government; they each have different law making processes, (some allowing popular initiative), and they represent three very different same-sex marriage outcomes (Crehan, 2013: 8). In terms of population, I would add, California ranks first in the country with 36,457,549; Massachusetts is thirteenth with 6,437,193; and Colorado is twenty-second with 4,753,377.

The other big question then is: Why has the American gay rights movement achieved success on some public policy issues but not others? In addressing the issue, Steven Boutcher informs us that in *Same Sex, Different Politics*, Gary Mucciaroni has provided a nuanced framework that incorporates both public opinion and the structure of political institutions as key mediating mechanisms in his analysis of six different LGBT (Lesbian, Gay, Bisexual, and Transgender) policy issues: marriage and partnership benefits, adoption, sodomy repeal, military service, hate crime laws and civil rights such as employment discrimination (Boutcher, 2010: 1503). Mucciaroni, we are told, argues that each policy issue contains a different set of politics and is "marked by a distinct struggle and by political and institutional differences that are critical for determining success" (Boutcher, 2010: 1503). For example, Boutcher goes on to demonstrate, the institutional forces surrounding the struggle to repeal "don't ask don't tell" are very different than the politics that surround the passage of hate crime laws. While seemingly simple, Steven Boutcher thinks this comparative insight provides a framework that proves to be crucial for understanding why gay rights advocates are successful on certain issues but not others (2010: 1503).

Martino-Taylor (2008) would want to ascribe the difficulty with 'don't ask don't tell' to the very secretive and undemocratic culture of the military, a culture that sees the social autism created by the same military establishment as very normal. For instance, she sees the secrecy of the military as creating a new social autism which encompasses a societal misunderstanding of reality, a minimal appreciation of danger, and a suppression of full and open debate regarding the manufacture, use, and testing of biological and chemical weaponry on humans, a testing especially based on race and class (Martino-Taylor, 2008: 41-48). By identifying those activities that are hidden behind a shroud of secrecy, her hope was that society can then compare the moral universe of the Military-Industrial-Academic (MIA) Complex to that of a democratic society, with society being able to challenge the parameters of the MIA's powerful local moral universe and remedy the social autism.

Yet other authors would think there is a better way out of the mess – looking at same-sex marriage as a religious right. Although the government does not inhibit churches from sanctifying same-sex unions, according to some critics, it does not give these unions the same legal status as other marriages. In this way, they conclude, the denial of equal marriage rights to same-sex couples violates the religious liberty of churches and religious people who support gay marriage out of religious conviction, as well as non-religious citizens (DeLaet and Caufield, 2008: 300). The lawyer who revolutionized American constitutional law would rather put it this way: "The way I understand the respondents' argument, the atheists are in, the agnostics are in, the communists are in, the religion [same-sex couple] is not in" (Toobin, 2011: 327). That might not be acceptable because, although religion couldn't be privileged under the Constitution, it couldn't be penalized either (Toobin, 2011: 327). After a lengthy demonstration of the cases (DeLaet and Caufield, 2008: 300-305) and recognizing as well its possible criticisms (DeLaet and Caufield, 2008: 315-318), DeLaet and Caufield advanced the position that:

a religious rights framework offers a potentially compelling strategic complement to equal rights arguments in the case of gay marriage. An equal protection argument restricts the focus of the question to the individual rights of those who wish to be married. While we believe this is an important social, moral, and political question to address, layering equal protection claims with religious liberties claims helps us to recognize that we are, in fact, debating individual rights as well as the rights of faith-based communities. Thus, advocates for gay marriage may find that framing gay marriage as a religious right has greater potential for changing the legal landscape in the United States than a legal strategy relying exclusively on equal rights arguments [DeLaet and Caufield, 2008: 305]

Even if a religious rights framework does not gain legal traction in the courts, its proponents believe that it provides us with a unique lens for viewing the debate over gay marriage in the United States that could change the way we think and talk about this issue. Denial of equal marriage rights to same-sex couples not only involves discrimination against same-sex couples and their families—it also constitutes religious establishment (DeLaet and Caufield, 2008: 320). As previously seen, Canada's gays and lesbians face few or none of these legal

160

battles since homosexuality has been legalized in this country that would be claiming multiculturalism but regards polygamy as one of the worst crimes on earth. I know many children of African Muslims who are going through hell here in Montreal because their own mothers could not be here with them since their father is only allowed to be here with only one of his four or so wives. Yet, Canada sees nothing wrong with that; instead preferring to even legalize homosexuals' RIGHT TO ADOPT CHILDREN! I have nothing against these gays and lesbians. But I am not afraid to ask the fundamental questions that many are shying away from posing: WHERE WOULD THESE CHILDREN (including the Homosexuals themselves) COME FROM (for them to adopt) IF EVERY ONE ELSE WAS LIKE THE HOMOSEXUALS? Why has the COPYOCRACY refused this time to DO THE COPYING FROM AMERICA? If HOMOSEXUALITY HAS BECOME PART OF MULTICULTURALISM, then WHAT IS THERE TO LOGICALLY KEEP POLYGAMY OUT OF MULTICULTURALISM? Isn't that just part of the Hypocrisy called multicultural Canada?

Conclusion

The conclusion is that there is no conclusion. I leave the answer to whether or not Canadian immigration, employment, and welfare policies should be revamped entirely as that of the readers who have been provided with adequate facts here and in Fossungu (2014b) to be able to make up their own minds.

But if you insist, as I can see you are doing, on knowing where I stand, then I say YES: if not for the sake of the adult capagivistic victims and other sex lovers like polygamists, then DO IT CANADA FOR THE SAKE OF THE CHILDREN AND THEIR FUTURE. As I have said, the family courts of this country have proven to be perfect tools in the hands of scheming women. It is about time these courts wake up and stop assisting fake victims to endlessly continue to ruin the future of innocent children. A mother who is determined to destroy or limit the partner's chances of progress does not at all care about the children except for the money their presence with her (called full custody of them) brings in. Does a mother also have the child at all in mind when she argues unnecessary with the child's day-care provider? I hope that I have presented some plain facts in this book that would expose some of the inconsistencies in Canadian policies and the myriad of contrivances that some of those (from other cultures) who arrive in Canada employ to exploit the generous peoples of Canada.

The expectation is that the authorities can now be able to take some appropriate measures to ensure that the interests of voiceless children are put first and protected against machinations from whatever quarters. Also, the operation of the current regulations in Canada is not smart, the more especially with the issue of permanent residence. The institution of the clean and clear proposals here in regard of foreign students, would not only benefit Canadian academic institutions, they would also prevent the predicament of children that are brought into this world solely as intimidation and money-getting devices. If in this way this book helps in cutting down the number of such children in Canada (and elsewhere), it would have attained one of its main objectives.

Bibliography

Achal, Lawrence Kyaligonza and Raymond Chegedua Tangonyire (2012), *Economic Behaviour As If Others Too Had Interests* (Bamenda: Langaa RPCIG).

Akokpari, John K. (2001) "Globalisation and the Challenges for the African State" *Nordic Journal of African Studies* 10:2: 188-209.

Alhassen, Maytha and Ahmed Shihab-Eldin (eds.) (2012), *Demanding Dignity: Young Voices from the Front Lines of the Arab Revolutions* (Ashland, OR: White Cloud Press).

Baker, Raymond W. , (2012) "The Paradox of Islam's Future" in Daniel Byman and Marylena Mantas (eds.), *Religion, Democracy, and Politics in the Middle East* (New York: The Academy of Political Science), 197-239.

Black, Amy E., Douglas L Koopman and Larycia A. Hawkins (eds.) (2011), *Religion and American Politics: Classic and Contemporary Perspectives* (New York: Longman).

Bogart, W.A. (1994) *Courts and Country: The Limits of Litigation and the Social and Political Life in Canada* (Toronto: Oxford University Press).

Boutcher, Steven A. (2010) "Book Review of Gary Mucciaroni's *Same-Sex, Different Politics: Success and Failure in the Struggle over Gay Rights* (Chicago: The University of Chicago Press, 2008)" *Social Forces* 88:3: 1503-1504.

Brooks, Stephen (1996) *Canadian Democracy: An Introduction* (2nd edition) (Toronto: Oxford University Press).

Byman, Daniel (2012a) "Overview: A New Middle East?" in Daniel Byman and Marylena Mantas (eds.), *Religion, Democracy, and Politics in the Middle East* (New York: The Academy of Political Science), vii-xii.

Byman, Daniel (2012b) "Regime Change in the Middle East: Problems and Prospects" in Daniel Byman and Marylena

Mantas (eds.), *Religion, Democracy, and Politics in the Middle East* (New York: The Academy of Political Science), 59-80.

Call, Charles T (2008) "The Fallacy of the 'Failed State'" *Third World Quarterly* 29:8: 1491-1507.

Campbell, David E. and Robert D. Putnam (2012) "God and Caesar in America: Why Mixing Religion and Politics Is Bad for Both" *Foreign Affairs* 91:34-43.

Colding, Rosetta (2013) "Fossungu's *Africans in Canada: Blending Canadian and African Lifestyles?*" available at http://www. examiner. com/review/fossungu-s-africans-canada-blending-canadian-and-african-lifestyles?cid=rss (last visited on 24 September 2013).

Collier, Paul and Juan William Gunning (2013) "Why Has Africa Grown Slowly?" in Patrick H. O'Neil and Ronald Rogowski, *Essential Readings in Comparative Politics* (4th edition) (New York: W. W. Norton & Company), 553-571.

Crehan, Margaret Gram (2013) *The Divided States of America: A Comparative Case Study of Same-Sex Marriage in the United States* (Ph. D. Dissertation, Northeastern University).

Cunningham, Maurice T. (2005) "Catholics and the ConCon: The Church's Response to the Massachusetts Gay Marriage Decision" *Journal of Church and State* 47:1: 19-42.

Dabashi, Hamid (2012) *The Arab Spring: The End of Postcolonialism* (London: Zed Books).

Daloglu, Begum (2014) "Turkey's Road to EU Membership in the Aftermath of the Arab Spring Uprisings" (Major Research Paper for the Award of Master of Arts – Political Science, defended on October 9, 2014, University of Windsor).

Dassault, Stéphane (2014) "Une charcuterie faisait son bœuf haché avec 3% de porc" *Journal de Montréal* (26 septembre), 7.

Debrix, François (1998) "Deterritorialised Territories, Borderless Borders: The New Geography of International Medical Assistance" *Third World Quarterly* 19:5: 827-846.

DeLaet, Debra L. and Rachel Paine Caufield (2008) "Gay
Marriage as a Religious Right: Reframing the Legal Debate
over Gay Marriage in the United States" *Polity* 40:3: 297-
320.

Eagleton, Terry (2011) "In Praise of Marx" *Chronicle* (April 10)
available @ http://www. chronicle. com/article/In-Praise-
of-Marx/127027/

Edsall, Thomas B. (2013) "Does Rising Inequality Make Us
Hardhearted?" *The New York Times* (December 10),
http://www. nytimes. com/2013/12/11/opinion/does-
rising-inequality.

Esposito, John L. (2012) "The Future of Islam and U. S. -
Muslim Relations" in Daniel Byman and Marylena Mantas
(eds.), *Religion, Democracy, and Politics in the Middle East* (New
York: The Academy of Political Science, 2012), 159-195.

Ferguson, James (2006) *Global Shadows: Africa in the Neoliberal
World Order* (Durham: Duke University Press).

Ferguson, Michaele L (2010) "Choice Feminism and the Fear
of Politics" *Perspectives on Politics* 8:1: 247-253.

Ferguson, Niall (2008) *The Ascent of Money: A Financial History of
the World* (New York: Penguin Books).

Fletcher, Ian (2011a) "The Famous (and Almost Never
Understood) Theory of Comparative Advantage" @
http://huntingtonpost. com/ian-fletcher-the-famous-and-
almost-nev_b_845930. Html.

_____ (2011b) "The Theory That's Killing America's
Economy – And Why It's Wrong" @
http://huntingtonpost. com/ian-fletcher-the-theory-thats-
killing_b_846452. html?ir=Politics.

Fombad, Charles Manga (2005) "The Separation of Powers
and Constitutionalism in Africa: The Case of Botswana"
25:2*Boston College Third World Law Journal*: 301-42.

_____ (2003) "Protecting Constitutional Values in
Africa: A Comparison of Botswana and Cameroon" 36:1
Comparative and International Law of Southern Africa: 83-105.

Fossungu, Peter Ateh-Afac (2014a) *Africa's Anthropological Dictionary on Love and Understanding: Marriage and the Tensions of Belonging in Cameroon* (Bamenda: Langaa RPCIG).

_____ (2014b) *The HISOFE Dictionary of Midnight Politics: Expibasketical Theories on Afrikentication and African Unity* (Bamenda: Langaa RPCIG).

_____ (2013a) *Africans in Canada: Blending Canadian and African Lifestyles?* (Bamenda: Langaa RPCIG).

_____ (2013b) *Understanding Confusion in Africa: The Politics of Multiculturalism and Nation-building in Cameroon* (Bamenda: Langaa RPCIG).

_____ (2013c) *Democracy and Human Rights in Africa: The Politics of Collective Participation and Governance in Cameroon* (Bamenda: Langaa RPCIG).

Furlong, Paul and David Marsh (2010) "A Skin Not a Sweater: Ontology and Epistemology in Political Science", in David Marsh and Gerry Stoker (eds.), *Theory and Methods in Political Science (3rd ed.)* (London: Palgrave Macmillan), 184-211.

Gagnon, Jean-Paul (2011) "Nation-State or Country-State: How Do We Discuss Belonging in an Age of Fluidity?" *Open Democracy* (April 12) @ http://opendemocracy. net-

Gardinier, Michael (2011) "Nation-State or Country-State: Response to Gagnon from the UK" *Open Democracy* (April 12) @ http://opendemocracy. net-

Göymen, Korel (2007) "Interaction of Democracy and Islam in Turkey" in Zoya Hasan (ed.), *Democracy in Muslim Societies: The Asian Experience* (New Delhi: Sage Publications India Ltd.), 219-255.

Grosby, Steven (2005) "The Fate of Nationality" *Society* (Jan-Feb), 15-20.

Haddad, Bassam, Rosie Bsheer, and Ziad Abu Rish (eds.), (2012) *The Dawn of the Arab Uprisings: End of an Old Order?* (London: Pluto Press).

Hasan, Zoya (2007) "Introduction" in Hasan, Zoya (ed.), *Democracy in Muslim Societies: The Asian Experience* (New Delhi: Sage Publications India Ltd.), 11-45.

Hiebert, Daniel (2003) "A Borderless World: Dream or Nightmare?" *ACME: An International E-Journal for Critical Geographies* 2:2: 188-193.

Hopkin, Jonathan (2010) "The Comparative Method" in David Marsh and Gerry Stoker (eds.), *Theory and Methods in Political Science* (3^{rd}ed.). (London: Palgrave Macmillan), 285-307.

Hutchison, Bruce (1943) *The Unknown Country: Canada and Her People* (Toronto: Longman, Green & Co).

James, Harold (2009) *The Creation and Destruction of Value: The Globalization Cycle* (Cambridge, Mass.: Harvard University Press).

John, Peter (2010) "Quantitative Methods" in David Marsh and Gerry Stoker (eds.), *Theory and Methods in Political Science* (3^{rd}ed.). (London: Palgrave Macmillan), 267-284.

Jungling, Laurie A. (2007) *Faithful Calling: A Relational Theo-Ethical Approach to the Lutheran Concept of Vocation and Marriage* (Ph. D. Dissertation, Berkeley, California).

Knutson, Katherine E. (2011) "Religion and Public Policy" in Amy E. Black, Douglas L. Koopman, and Larycia A. Hawkins (eds.) *Religion and American Politics: Classical and Contemporary Perspectives* (New York: Longman), 355-364.

Lawler, Phil (2013) "Homosexual Network at the Vatican, Yes; Reason for the Pope's Resignation, No" February 22, 2013, available @ http://www. catholicculture. org/commentary/otn. cfm?id=968.

Lindorff, Dave (2013) "About Time American Idiocy and Paranoia Over Marxism Got Called Out" *The Nation of Change* available @ http://www. nationofchange. org-About-Time-American-Idiocy.

Lust-Okar, Ellen (2005), *Structuring Conflict in the Arab World: Incumbents, Opponents, and Institutions* (Cambridge: Cambridge University Press).

169

Marsh, David and Gerry Stoker, eds. (2010), *Theory and Methods in Political Science (3rd ed.).* (London: Palgrave Macmillan).

Martino-Taylor, Lisa (2008) "The Military-Industrial-Academic Complex and a New Social Autism" *Journal of Political and Military Sociology* 36:1:37-52.

Matar, Matar Ebrahim (2012) "Battling Bahrain's Crimes of Humanity" in Maytha Alhassen and Ahmed Shihab-Eldin (eds.), *Demanding Dignity: Young Voices from the Front Lines of the Arab Revolutions* (Ashland, OR: White Cloud Press), 129-141.

McGarvie, Mark Douglas (2000) *One Nation under Law: America's Early National Struggles to Separate Church and State* (Ph. D. Dissertation, Department of History, Indiana University).

Mentan, Tatah (2013a) *Assault on Paradise: Perspectives on Globalization and Class Struggles in Africa* (Bamenda: Langaa RPCIG).

_____ (2013b) *Democracy for Breakfast Unveiling Mirage Democracy in Contemporary Africa* (Bamenda: Langaa RPCIG).

_____ (2012) *Socialism: The Only Practical Alternative to Contemporary Capitalism* (Bamenda: Langaa RPCIG).

Nahar, Snigdha (2008) "Sovereign Equality Principle in International Law" *Global Politician* available @ http://globalpolitician. com/default. asp?24351-international-law.

Najem, Tom Pierre (2003) "State Power and Democratization in North Africa: Developments in Morocco, Algeria, Tunisia, and Libya" in Amin Saikal and Albrecht Schnabel (eds.), *Democratization in the Middle East: Experiences, Struggles, Challenges* (New York: United Nations University Press), 183-201.

Oliver, Michèle (2001) "Impact of the Arab Springs: Is Democracy Emerging as a Human Right in Africa?" @http://www. defenceweb. co. za/index. php?view=article

Oloka-Onyango, Joseph (2005) "Who's Watching 'Big Brother'? Globalization and the Protection of Cultural Rights in Present Day Africa" *Human Rights Quarterly* 27:4: 1245-1273.

Owen, Roger (2000) *State, Power and Politics in the Making of the Modern Middle East* (2nd edition) (New York: Routledge).

Owen, Roger (2012) "Foreword – Jadaliya: Archiving the Revolution" in Bassam Haddad, Rosie Bsheer, and Ziad Abu Rish (eds.), *The Dawn of the Arab Uprisings: End of an Old Order?* (London: Pluto Press), x-xvii.

Paasi, Anssi (2009) "Bounded Spaces in a 'Borderless World': Border Studies, Power and the Anatomy of Territory" *Journal of Power* 2:2: 213-234.

Patrikios, Stratos (2008) "American Republican Religion? Disentangling the Causal Link between Religion and Politics in the US" *Political Behavior* 30: 367-389.

Posusney, Marsha Pripstein (2004) "Enduring Authoritarianism: Middle East Lessons for Comparative Theory" *Comparative Politics* 36:2: 127-138.

Pratt, Nicola Christine (2007) *Democracy and Authoritarianism in the Arab World* (Boulder, CO: Lynne Rienner Publishing Inc.).

Putnam, Robert D. and David E. Campbell (2012) *American Grace: How Religion Divides and Unites Us* (New York: Simon and Schuster).

Randall, Vicky (2010) "Feminism" in David Marsh and Gerry Stoker (eds.), *Theory and Methods in Political Science* (3rd ed.). (London: Palgrave Macmillan), 114-135.

Rodrik, Dani (2010) *The Globalization Paradox – Democracy and the Future of the World Economy* (New York: W. W. Norton).

Ross, Michael L. (2011) "Will Oil Drown the Arab Spring? Democracy and the Resource Curse" *Foreign Affairs* (September/October 2011), 2-7. http/search. proquest. com/printviewfile?accountid=14789

Said, Edward W. (2001) "The Clash of Ignorance" *The Nation* (October 22) available @ http://www. the nation. com/doc/2001said/print

Saikal, Amin (2003) "Democracy and Peace in Iran and Iraq" in Amin Saikal and Albrecht Schnabel (eds.), *Democratization in the Middle East: Experiences, Struggles, Challenges* (New York: United Nations University Press, 2003), 166-182.

Saikal, Amin and Albrecht Schnabel (eds.), (2003) *Democratization in the Middle East: Experiences, Struggles, Challenges* (New York: United Nations University Press).

Saunders, Doug (2010) "The Middle East's New Emperor: Why the West Quietly Cheers Turkey's Rise" *The Globe and Mail* (Toronto) (May), http:licence/copyright. net/user/view/FreeUse-act?fuid=MTMSMDcyMzk%3D

Savage, Luiza Ch. (2014) "End of the Line" *Maclean's* 127:4 (March), 22-36, available at http://web. a. ebscohost. com/ehost/delivery?sid=a68eclef-cbbd-47b3-8bb2-aa465010f324%. . . pages 1-21.

Schnabel, Albrecht (2003) "A Rough Journey: Nascent Democratization in the Middle East", in Amin Saikal and Albrecht Schnabel (eds.), *Democratization in the Middle East: Experiences, Struggles, Challenges* (New York: United Nations University Press), 1-22.

Smidt, Corwin (2011) "Making Sense of the American Religious Landscape" in Amy E. Black, Douglas L. Koopman, and Larycia A. Hawkins (eds.) *Religion and American Politics: Classical and Contemporary Perspectives* (New York: Longman), 106-113.

Smiley, Donald (1992) "Courts, Legislatures, and the Protection of Human Rights" in F.L. Morton (ed.) *Law, Politics and the Judicial Process in Canada* (2nd edition) (Calgary: University of Calgary Press), 462-464.

Smith, Miriam (2005) "The Politics of Same-Sex Marriage in Canada and the United States" *Political Science & Politics* 38:2: 225-228.

Song, Yin (2009) *Cultural Hybridization: Rethinking Globalization in China and the U. S.* (Master of Arts Thesis, Department of American Studies, The University at Buffalo, State University of New York).

Sparke, Matthew (2013) *Introducing Globalization: Ties, Tensions, and Uneven Integration* (Maden, MA: Wiley-Blackwell.

Stanley, Liam (2012) "Research and Analysis: Rethinking the Definition and Role of Ontology in Political Science" *Politics* 32:2: 93-99.

Thoreson, Ryan (2013) "Beyond Equality: The Post-Apartheid Counternarrative of Trans and Intersex Movements in South Africa" *African Affairs* 112:449: 646-665.

Whyte, John D. (1992) "On Not Standing for Notwithstanding" in F.L. Morton (ed.) *Law, Politics and the Judicial Process in Canada* (2nd edition) (Calgary: University of Calgary Press), 467-474.

Sullivan, Andrew (2011) "Why Gay Marriage Is Good for Straight America: As Same-sex Couples March Down the Aisle in New York, the Author Reflects on his own Life, Love, and Pursuit of Happiness" *Newsweek* 158:4.

Tessier, Mark (2002) "Islam and Democracy in the Middle East: The Impact of Religious Orientations on Attitudes toward Democracy in Four Arab Countries" *Comparative Politics* 34:3: 337-354.

Toal, Gerard (1999) "Borderless World? Problematising Discourses of Deterritorialisation" *Geopolitics* 4:2: 139-154.

Toft, Monica Duffy (2007) "The Myth of the Borderless World: Refugees and Repatriation Policy" *Conflict Management and Peace Science* 24: 139-157.

Toobin, Jeffrey (2011) "The Nine: Inside the Secret World of the Supreme Court (2007)" in Amy E. Black, Douglas L. Koopman, and Larycia A. Hawkins (eds.) *Religion and American Politics: Classical and Contemporary Perspectives* (New York: Longman), 324-327.

Wahlbeck, Paul (2011) "Judicial Decision Making and Religion Cases" in Amy E. Black, Douglas L. Koopman, and Larycia A. Hawkins (eds.) *Religion and American Politics: Classical and Contemporary Perspectives* (New York: Longman), 313-321.

Westbrook, Neil P. (2010) *The Institution of Marriage and the Role of the Local Church: A Study at Neel Road Baptist Church in Salisbury, North Carolina* (Ph. D. Dissertation, McAfee School of Theology, Atlanta, Georgia).

Westley, F. R. (1992) "Religion" in James T. Teevan, Jr. (ed.) *Introduction to Sociology: A Canadian Focus* (4th edition) (Scarborough, Ont.: Prentice-Hall), 329-366.

Wexelblat, David (2012) "Trojan Horse or Much Ado About Nothing? Analyzing the Religious Exemptions in New York's Marriage Equality Act" *Journal of Gender, Social Policy & the Law* 20:4: 961-993.

Wiktorowicz, Quintan and Karl Kaltenthaler (2012) "The Rationality of Radical Islam" in Daniel Byman and Marylena Mantas (eds.), *Religion, Democracy, and Politics in the Middle East* (New York: The Academy of Political Science), 109-133.

Zibakalam, Sadegh (2007) "The History of the Democratic Movement in Iran in the 20th Century" in Hasan, Zoya (ed.), *Democracy in Muslim Societies: The Asian Experience* (New Delhi: Sage Publications India Ltd.), 112-127.

www.ingramcontent.com/pod-product-compliance
Lightning Source LLC
Chambersburg PA
CBHW071024280326
41935CB00011B/1475